WHAT'S SO GOOD ABOUT TOUGH TIMES?

WHAT'S SO GOOD ABOUT TOUGH TIMES?

STORIES *of* PEOPLE REFINED *by* DIFFICULTY

JOE WHEELER

WATERBROOK
PRESS

WHAT'S SO GOOD ABOUT TOUGH TIMES?
PUBLISHED BY WATERBROOK PRESS
2375 Telstar Drive, Suite 160
Colorado Springs, Colorado 80920
A division of Random House, Inc.

Scripture taken from the *Holy Bible, New International Version*®. NIV®. Copyright © 1973, 1978, 1984
by International Bible Society. Used by permission of Zondervan Publishing House. All rights reserved.

Woodcut illustrations are from the library of Joe Wheeler.

ISBN 1-57856-321-6

Copyright © 2001 by Joe Wheeler

Published in association with the literary agency of Alive Communications, Inc., 7680 Goddard Street,
Suite 200, Colorado Springs, CO 80920.

Library of Congress Cataloging-in-Publication Data
What's so good about tough times? : stories of people refined by difficulty / [compiled]
by Joe Wheeler.— 1st ed.
    p. cm. — (Forged in the fire series ; #1)
    Includes bibliographical references.
    ISBN 1-57856-321-6
        1. Christian life. 2. Suffering—Religious aspects—Christianity. I. Wheeler, Joe L., 1936- II. Series.

BV4909 .W48 2001
248.8'6—dc21

                                                                          2001035227

Printed in the United States of America
2001—First Edition

10 9 8 7 6 5 4 3 2 1

As I thought about who in my life has gone through tough times the longest, one name kept coming back to me. Many years ago she was told she was a brittle diabetic. She didn't know what that abstract term meant then, but she does now. Since she and her steadfast husband, Marvin, were both students of mine, we have remained in steady contact through the years. She has faced illness after illness, hospital after hospital, for as long as I've known her. Each year another section of her body closes down on her. Her career dreams, which once gleamed so brightly, are all gone now. Amazingly, she remains joyful each day, accepting each day as a gift from God, as in love with life and its beauty as ever. She revels in sitting on the beaches of the Pacific and filling her soul with its ever-changing beauty and grandeur.

Thus it is that I dedicate this book vicariously through her to all those millions of brave men, women, and children (and their supporting families) who daily battle this inexorable enemy, diabetes—and to one heroic woman specifically:

CORRIE JOY WHITNEY

OF

CRESCENT CITY, CALIFORNIA

CONTENTS

PART II: HOPE

PART III: HEALING

GOD'S GREAT GIFT—
TOUGH TIMES

My siblings and I have had many a chuckle out of Mom, "who'd drive a hundred miles to save a dime." It wasn't until I became a history major and studied in depth the Great Depression of the 1930s that I began to better understand my mother's extreme frugality.

In 1928, America's economy was roaring, and everyone seemed to think it would only get better. At a time when it was never easier to buy stocks on ever-smaller margins, millions of people—from millionaires to stenographers—invested heavily as if there were no tomorrow.

But the end came suddenly and without warning. It began on October 24, 1929—known forever after as Black Thursday—and continued its downward plunge through October 29—Black Tuesday. Frantic efforts to stabilize the market and halt the free fall were met by equally frantic efforts to *sell—must sell—at any price!*

In Washington, the Federal Reserve Board went into continuous session, not even stopping to eat, but could do nothing. Nine billion was lost on Black Tuesday alone; in two short weeks: thirty billion. Panic gripped the nation. In New York, desperate investors besieged their brokers' offices, each with its glass-domed ticker unit that typed out the dizzying descent of their fortunes. On the streets, ambulance sirens wailed, speeding to the sites of one suicide after another. Overnight, millionaires became paupers and could not come up with the money demanded by their brokers. Other investors were poor to begin with. Now they were not only broke; they were also in debt for more than they could ever hope to earn. There were no credit cards, no unemployment benefits, no food stamps, no disability income, no Medicare, no Social Security retirement income. Either you had money or you didn't. Not even bankruptcy was an option, for in that time to declare bankruptcy was to proclaim oneself unprincipled—a stigma worse than death itself.

As day after day, week after week, month after month, and year after year passed, things only got worse. Wry signs of the times blamed President Hoover for the financial crisis: "Hoover flags" (pockets emptied and turned inside out), "Hoover blankets" (newspapers covering park bench indigents), and "Hoovervilles" (makeshift shantytowns where the down-and-outers struggled to stay alive).

By the time 1931 drew to a close, of the total 122 million Americans, five million were unemployed. Jobless rates in some areas approached 50 percent. More than two million people wandered across the country as vagrants. Four hundred banks had failed, and there was then no Federal Deposit Insurance Corporation. Everywhere one looked, once proud, self-sufficient men and women had been reduced to begging enough food so their families could survive another day. Not without reason were six words seared into American consciousness for all time: *Brother, can you spare a dime?*

Things got still worse. By January 1932, more than two thousand banks had failed, and thirteen million people were then out of work. The hourly wages of those "lucky enough" to still have jobs were slashed by 60 percent. State governments, bordering on bankruptcy themselves, could do little to help: at most, five dollars a week per family. Foreclosures were occurring at a staggering rate of one hundred thousand plus homes a month.

In November, desperate Americans tossed Hoover out of the White House and elected Franklin D. Roosevelt in his place. It was a sober nation that sat glued to radio sets for that inaugural address and heard Roosevelt tell them that "The only thing to fear is fear itself." Now fully 25 percent of the nation was without jobs, the national income was less than half what it had been three years before, five thousand banks had collapsed, and in that maelstrom nine million family savings and checking accounts had disappeared forever. And times continued tough, year after year, on through the decade.

That, of course, is why my mother is so frugal: she grew up during those terrible years, saw her father lose his fortune, and gave birth to me during the mid-1930s.

So what did people *do* during those terrible times? Surprisingly, for the most part their actions did not emulate the desperation of the times. Families gathered around their own as hens protect their chicks; churches did likewise. Since almost no one was exempt from destitution, all across America people helped people with what little they had. And men, women, and children everywhere called upon God for help, for courage, for comfort, for hope.

The Depression seasoned the timber of a people and created in it greatness and strength of character. From this desperate life arose the men and women who would rescue the world from Hitler,

Mussolini, and Tojo during World War II and who would rebuild the world afterward. Not until the good times roared back did America lose her ethical and spiritual moorings.

Are the good times worth the cost?

Are tough times as bad as we make them?

Have you ever really listened to survivors talk about that terrible Depression? They tell us about a people who had seen life reduced to its bare essentials: To daily survival. To family ties made stronger than ever before or since. To sacrifice and selflessness. To an understanding of the value of work and how demoralizing it is to lose the opportunity to earn one's daily bread. And to realize, paradoxically, that those terrible tough times were in reality "good days"—the *best* in fact (looking back through the rose-tinted glasses of memory) ever experienced, for they *endured,* they *made it through,* and strangest of all, they were happier then than they have ever been since.

Why is this? Can we make some sort of sense out of it?

GOOD TIMES ARE BAD; BAD ARE GOOD

It may seem preposterous, but there's a lot of truth in the contention that good times are bad and bad times are good, for the fact is that we rarely grow much during good times. When we look back on our past, what is it we ruefully discover? Yes, that we grew most during periods of trauma. I like the way Harry Moyle Tippett put it in his book *Live Happier:*

[God] brings the dawn out of the most dismal night. He makes our balmy springs and fruitful summers to succeed the bitter blasts of winter. Out of blustery, tempestuous March He makes way for our singing Aprils and our flowering Mays. Out of ten thousand storms He develops the giant redwood tree, and in the cloud forms His noblest symphony of color, the rainbow. Likewise out of forty years of banishment and obscurity God carved a Moses, out of cruel betrayal into the hands of aliens He molded the statesman Joseph; out of physical, mental, and spiritual suffering, He demonstrated the perfection of Job.[1]

Earlier in his monumental little book, Tippet pointed out that

Out of the darkness of Milton's blindness came that greatest of epics, *Paradise Lost*. The great oratorio, *The Messiah*, came out of Handel's worst days. His health and fortunes were at a low ebb. His right side was paralyzed and his money gone. He was being threatened with imprisonment for debt.... Wilberforce was so small physically that people called him a shrimp. It was a handicap that became an involuntary cross. His health was so wretched that he was constantly under medical care. But diminutive though he was he threw all there was of him into the fight against slavery in England and her colonies. In spite of great opposition this pygmy man was largely instrumental in stopping the evil he hated.[2]

If it's possible—even true—that hardship gives way to greatness, why do we try to shield our loved ones, especially our children, from all trauma and stress? We race through life pushing doors open for those dearest to us, only to belatedly discover that we produced spineless jellyfish in the process and destroyed their potential for

---

1. Harry Moyle Tippett, *Live Happier* (Washington, D.C.: Review and Herald, 1957), 80-1.
2. Tippett, *Live Happier*, 27.

both temporal and spiritual success. Or to use another metaphor, we set our loved ones upon the sea of life in ships of shallow draft: in smooth water, they sail fine, but a storm of any kind will sink them.

God does not want all our doors to be open; He wants some to be swollen shut so that it takes great effort to budge them. Some doors are more than difficult to open; they are double- and triple-bolted shut. God has intended that we suffer disappointment, frustration, and heartbreak—and He intends that we will persevere, will cease banging on the closed portals, and will search for another door—one that will open.

Tippet put it this way:

> God knows that the things we acquire too easily are
> lightly esteemed. Perhaps that is the reason He hides many
> a blessing from us. He hides Himself, therefore, in pain
> that we may know His healing. He hides His best gifts in
> baffling disciplines, that they may come forth with the glow
> of the eternal. He conceals His purposes from His righteous
> Jobs, that they may reveal them to His pleading Jacobs.
> "The kingdom of heaven is like unto treasure hid in a field,"
> Jesus said. God designed that our possession of it should be
> a continual quest, even to the dedication of all that
> we have.[3]

If we study the lives of men and women we consider great, invariably tough times play a major role in their life stories. Interestingly, the qualities a nation seeks in its leaders vary according to condi-

---

3. Harry Moyle Tippett, *Who Waits in Faith* (Washington, D.C.: Review and Herald, 1951), 53.

tions: In good times we'll elect a Chamberlain, in tough times a Churchill; in good times a Clinton, in tough times a Lincoln. Why is Lincoln our most beloved president—by far!—with FDR and Washington the only near seconds? Perhaps because all three men were early on seasoned in the crucible of pain, and came out with such evidence of greatness that when the nation experienced three of its darkest periods (the Revolutionary War, the Civil War, and from the Depression through World War II), it turned to them— men who had the qualities to guide it through. All three appealed to the finest in human nature, and all achieved the near impossible because they did not even consider failure to be a possibility.

We treat differently those who have been through hell and survived. I am reminded of students of mine who waited many hours to see Nelson Mandela, who had been imprisoned for twenty-six long years and yet emerged without vindictiveness. When I asked them what the experience was like, they could come up with no adequate answer—the closest being "I was so awed by the man that I just *stood* there, looking at him." Much of our admiration for Senator John McCain of Arizona stems from his having endured so many years of terrible treatment as a prisoner of war—we can't separate the man from what he has endured. F. C. Budlong put it this way:

Look into the face of a person who has fought no great temptation and endured no supreme sorrow, and you'll find little there to arouse your admiration. Look upon one who has weathered a great grief, like a mighty ocean liner ploughing through a tempest, and you'll observe strength and grace in every lineament.... The expression in your eye, the lines in your face, the quality of your smile, the tone of your voice, tell the story, without your being conscious of it, whether your soul has faced its Gethsemane with courage, or with shaming compromise and cowardly surrender.

Struggle and difficulty bring additional compensation: Without them we can no more appreciate the good times than trust-kid drones can appreciate a vacation, for how can you take a vacation from a vacation? Edwin Markham noted: "Defeat may serve as well as victory to shake the soul and let the glory out. When the great oak is straining in the wind, the boughs drink in new beauty, and the trunk sends down a deeper root on the windward side. Only the soul that knows the mighty grief can know the mighty rapture. Sorrow comes to stretch out spaces in the heart for joy."

So, if there is one clear conclusion we can reach from this short study, it is this: *Tough times are good for us.* Without them we stagnate and begin to die. Only during tough times do we grow. Failure to grow is to bring a tear to the eye of God. No greater failure can there be than to waste the daily opportunities God grants us, opportunities which, once squandered, can never be retrieved. God gives only today, this hour, this moment:

> The clock of life is wound but once
> And no man has the power
> To tell just when the hand will stop
> On what day—or what hour.
> Now is the only time you have
> So live it with a will.
> Don't wait until tomorrow,
> The hands may then be still.
> —Author Unknown

THE THREE *H*s

In this book are stories having to do with Heartache, Hope, and Healing. There is value in all intense living; the highs and lows are responsible for much of the drama, color, and contrast in our lives—otherwise we'd lead merely a zombyish, Prozac existence. But the lows impact us most of all.

America's greatest poetess, Emily Dickinson, was no stranger to inner agony; in fact, her greatest poetry was penned with the ink of anguish. Well she knew that it could not be feigned:

> I like a look of Agony
> Because I know it's true
> > —from "I Like a Look of Agony"

Pain, she postulated, is so all-consuming that it cannot coexist with anything else:

> Pain—has an Element of Blank—
> It cannot recollect
> When it began—or if there were
> A time when it was not
> > —"Pain Has an Element of Blank"

And Heartache is the tortuous trail we almost invariably travel alone. Only in this ultimate extremity do we at last shed our cloak of self-sufficiency. In our brokenness, we turn and find our Lord standing there.

He does not hand us baubles, pat answers, or a boulevard of escape. He does not because, having made us, He knows full well that we value all things proportionately to the pain they cost us. God, having in Him all the patience of One dwelling outside time, is willing to wait, wait until we are refined in the crucible of pain. No one has ever been exempt from that process, and none has ever achieved greatness without it. But God knows we find it difficult to suffer in darkness without a light to long toward. And so He created Hope, described by Dickinson in these words:

> 'Hope' is the thing with feathers—
> That perches in the soul—
> And sings the tune without the words—
> And never stops—at all—
>
> And sweetness—in the Gale—is heard—
> And sore must be the storm—
> That could abash the little Bird
> That kept so many warm—
>
> I've heard it in the chillest land—
> And on the strangest Sea—
> Yet, never, in Extremity
> It asked a crumb—of Me
>   —"Hope Is the Thing with Feathers"

Hope is often the *only* thing that gets us through heartbreak, for without it, we die. In fact, Alexandre Dumas père, in *The Three Musketeers,* concluded that "Hope is the last thing to die in the human heart."

Ultimately, healing comes to us, but slowly. Were it not so, were the price cheap, we would perversely repeat the same mistakes over and over. And even those closest to us, who perhaps tend to take us for granted, in those dark, dark days that are bathed with tears, learn to value us proportionately to the fragility of our cord of life and to the duration of our climb back to health. Every tiny step upward in the healing process is cause for rejoicing. Why God permits each siege of suffering, we know not, but someday we'll know the why. Dickinson put it this way:

> I shall know why—when Time is over—
> And I have ceased to wonder why—
> Christ will explain each separate anguish
> In the fair schoolroom of the sky—
>
> He will tell me what 'Peter' promised—
> And I—for wonder at his woe—
> I shall forget the drop of Anguish
> That scalds me now—that scalds me now!
> —"I Shall Know Why"

STORIES IN THIS COLLECTION

Between these two covers is as stellar a cast of authors as I've ever fielded, with the likes of Mark Twain, Harriet Lummis Smith, Margaret E. Sangster Jr., John Galsworthy, G. E. Wallace, and Abbie Farwell Brown; as well as contemporary authors our readers have already come to love, such as Arthur Gordon, Shirley Barksdale, and Arthur Milward.

Some of the stories have to do with accepting one's role in life, or what can't be changed: stories such as "Her Inside Face" and "Message from the Sea." Stories dealing directly with handicaps are

"The Making of Mike" and "My Son—Handicapped." Two of the stories have to do with renunciation and giving one's all: "The Ragged Cloak" and "The Dissolving of a Partnership." Two portray children suffering deeply, yet trying to make a difference: "The Death Disk" and "Two Candles for St. Anthony." Three deal with acceptance of one's tough times and willingness to make the best of what one has: "158 Spruce Street," "Hilda's Trousseau," and "Along Came Cynthia." Yet two others deal with resolution and eventual success after many tribulations: "The Wall of Silence" and "October Song." Another pair has to do with caring and service for others: "The Missing Word" and "The Red Geranium." One story, "Quality," has to do with doing one's best even when few appreciate or support you. "The Firing of Donald Capen" and "A Good Name or Great Riches" have to do with standing up for principle against great odds.

Readers will note that in order to give this collection a New England slant I have woven into the fabric of this introduction and my story, "October Song," the voices of that region's three most beloved poets: Longfellow, Dickinson, and Frost.

CODA

It is my prayer and my hope that this book will prove to be both a joy and a blessing to you. If you know of additional tough times stories with the same emotive power as these, I would deeply appreciate your sending me copies, with information about authorship, date, and place of earliest publication, if known. As I am editing collections of stories in other genres, I welcome stories outside this tough times genre as well.

If our responses from you are positive, we will consider another collection of tough times stories at a later date. I look forward to hearing from you, and you may reach me by writing to:

Joe L. Wheeler, Ph.D.
c/o WaterBrook Press
2375 Telstar Drive, Suite 160
Colorado Springs, CO 80920

PART I

HEARTACHE

Surely in vain have I kept my heart pure;
in vain have I washed my hands in innocence.
All day long I have been plagued;
I have been punished every morning.

PSALM 73:13-14

ALONE, YET NOT ALONE AM I

Henry Melchior Muhlenberg
with Regina Leininger and Maria Le Roy

Of stories having to do with mother love and survival against almost overwhelming odds, few are more gripping than this one, dating back to the bloody border days of the mid-1700s, a time when massacres such as this one were, sadly, all too common.

This narrative of my maternal ancestors is a composite pieced together from the Regina Leininger and Maria Le Roy transcripts, as well as the chronicle penned by the Rev. Henry M. Muhlenberg (1711-1787), founder of the Lutheran Church in America.

———

Sing for us, mutter," pleaded Regina, as the sycamore and pine crackled and flared against the back log in the rough stone fireplace of the lonely cabin.

"Ach, kinder, what shall I sing to you—a Schlaflied?"

She was a broad, strong woman, ruddy and handsome, with the buxom vigor that belonged to her hale German heredity and her life in the wilderness of the strange new world. Beside the rough pine table her husband used the evening's hearth light to repair a crude piece of harness. Around her were her children, two sons and as many daughters. The boys were in their teens, but self-reliant, with the air of pioneer boys who have already learned their lessons of woodcraft. The girls were children still. Regina was not yet ten years old, and Barbara, her sister, whose hand she held as she spoke, was only twelve.

Odd hands they were. Their thumbs were already flattened to a marked spatula from the twisting of flax, which filled every spare instant of their waking hours, except for this last interlude before they would bundle into the shut-in bunk that had been called a bed in Germany. Their mother had just such a hand marked with just such a thumb, grossly exaggerated. Hers had been acquired across the sea and would remain deformed until she died.

The hides drying on the cabin walls, and the skins comprising some of the garments of the boys and their father, were evidence of the substitutes these pioneers used for wool in this new country, where sheep were the easy prey of wolf and panther....

But good linen the careful German housewife must have, and her daughters were growing up to the domestic virtues under expert guidance.... Men, in those times, looked at a girl's thumb for just such an unnatural flattening.

Regina, who was the pet of the family, pondered her mother's suggestion for a minute.

"Oh, mutter," she said, "sing what thou dost always sing— *Allein, Doch Nich Allein Ein Ich.*"

Her clear, blue eyes on the flames, and her full maternal bosom swelling as she took the higher notes of the old hymn, the pioneer's wife intoned with the girls adding low their sweet sopranos and the boys humming to their father's rumbling bass:

Alone, yet not alone am I,
Though in this solitude so drear,
I feel my Saviour always nigh;
He comes the weary hours to cheer,
I am with Him, and He with me—
E'en here alone I cannot be.

She sang the hymn through, and a blessed peace seemed to fill the tiny cabin, its door made fast by the great crossbar of oak, its one window, shuttered with a two-inch plank, barred too.

"Bed now, kinder!" she commanded. "I must go to the mill in the morning."

But Regina pleaded, as a child will. "Ach, mutter, the fire isn't dead yet. Sing again. Let's sing 'Jesus, Evermore I Love.'"

So the mother sang that hymn too. And again the family joined their voices to hers in the music that was a prayer—a prayer, like the first, of the kind whose need none knew better than these adventurers into a region which only the most needy and the most daring penetrated.

"Nun, schnell!" she cried, briskly. "Come, vater"—to her husband—"put it aside. It is early morning tomorrow."

Leininger…hung his scrap of harness on a nail. The embers flickered and fell away against the back log. The wilderness, with its one small group of human beings, sank into its quiet slumber, prelude to one of the most gory Indian massacres Pennsylvania's border history ever knew.

We pride ourselves now on our fair treatment of our early savages. But the traditions of the tribes carried long and bitter grudges born of the white man's double dealing and treachery, and the day Frau Leininger had appointed for riding with the grist to the mill was the day the red man had chosen for one of a bloody reckoning.

The Leiningers' home was near the present town of Selinsgrove, on the edge of the line run by the English as the boundary of the land they had acquired from the Six Nations by the Albany Treaty of July 6, 1754. The boundary lay about a mile from the juncture of Penn's Creek with the Susquehanna River. In August of 1754 the Delaware Indians, at a conference they'd demanded, denounced the treaty on the ground that under the tribal agreement, the Six Nations had no right to give away that territory without their consent. The English paid no heed to the protest, but went ahead and sold settlers' rights to a score and more families. Before the autumn was past the Leiningers and their fellow pioneers had made their homes along Penn's Creek. They were Europe's furthest outposts in its relentless seizure of a continent.

Braddock's defeat meant the Indians' chance to recover their own. The Delawares cast their lot with the French, whose campaign required immediate control of the ground where the two branches of the Susquehanna join at Sunbury. Adjoining the territory, owned by the Delawares, it would give them control of the approaches and operations against eastern and southern Pennsylvania.

The English countered by erecting Fort Augusta, which held the French at bay. But the Indians, fiercely resentful of their wrongs, carried on the invasion along their own sudden, sanguine lines of campaign. The tale of their first unheralded onslaught, the brunt of which was born by the hapless pioneers along Penn's Creek, long thrilled fireside groups with horror....

When the Leiningers rose on the morning of October 16, 1755, a year after they'd built their cabin in the wilderness, they guessed nothing of the impending disaster. For all the presence of other settlers in the region, the solitude about them seemed absolute. A couple of dozen cabins scattered over the leagues might have been so many birds' nests.

Breakfast, substantial as the German pioneers liked it and the game-filled land provided, delayed the careful housewife's departure. She must be sure that Barbara and Regina would wash all the dishes well; that they would ready the house while she was away; that they knew what to prepare for dinner, should she be delayed in her return. One of the boys must go with her, the other could stay at home helping his father. At last all her routine was arranged.

"Good-bye!" she called cheerfully, as she and her boy struck into the path through the forest.

Some miles away, in even more leisurely fashion, fast had been broken around their campfires by the hundreds of grim Delawares, with the Shawnees, their allies. The warriors even made more elaborate toilettes, adding touches of their war paint until an unearthly hideousness distorted the pitiless hawk look of their dusky features.

Their tomahawks in hand, every one fitting accurately his tread into the steps of the others, they sped naked and shadowlike toward Penn's Creek.

The series of surprises was complete. Like the Leiningers, none of the settlers suspected their doom until it leaped, with blood-curdling war whoops, upon them. Leininger and his son, each seized by a couple of savages, were tomahawked and scalped in the clearing of their little cabin, while the girls stared, shrieking from where they stood in the midst of their household tasks. In a space no longer than a minute, the two sisters, from happiness and freedom, were transformed into captives and slaves.

Just as they were, Barbara and Regina were bound and dragged into the forest by the Indians, their last glance back at their home telling them that it was in flames. As they progressed, they described pillars of smoke, the burning homes of their neighbors. After a while their captors halted, flinging them to the ground. Then, leaving several braves to guard them, the others sped away to fresh slaughter.

From time to time Indians arrived, dragging more captives to the rendezvous. Soon the sisters realized what must be the extent, and also the appalling nature, of the massacre. It was deadly ominous that among all the prisoners there were only children, many of them babies scarcely able to walk. Most of them were girls, and where boys had been spared a captive's fate they were very young. Women and men—all who were past the age which the Indians believed them capable of complete absorption into the tribal life— had been ruthlessly tomahawked and scalped.

Several days passed, while the sisters, in company of the ever-increasing number of child prisoners, remained under guard and the country for miles around was laid waste with fire and tomahawk. Braves carried in terrified children, whose faces were blood-stained from the scalps of their mothers, which hung from their captors' belts. At first, throughout this frightened multitude of children, a low whimpering prevailed. But the blows that were sure to fall on anyone who murmured ere long reduced them to a frightened stillness, and they lay or sat, horror-eyed, while their bodies began to waste from the hunger they endured throughout their waiting.

At length, when all the Indians concerned in the massacre had assembled with their child prisoners, the trail was taken up toward the lands of the Delawares and the Shawnees. Barbara and Regina, like the other girls whose years and strength made it possible for them to carry burdens, were given little ones to carry on their backs, where the babies were strapped securely.

Steadily westward, for hundreds of miles, that terrible trail was followed. From the start, any line of progress that bore a resemblance of a pathway was avoided. The Indians were only too aware that once word of their raid was spread, pursuit would be instant. They were making it as dubious and difficult as possible.

The tramping children were all barefoot, yet unused to such rough traveling. The way led through mire and swamps, among the underbrush and briars, over brush and sharp flint. Yet not for a moment did the savages check the speed of their retreat. The girl who fell with her burden was whipped like a tired pony. Those tender feet were soon cut and torn to the very bones, and the tendons in some were severed. Scarcely a day had gone by before the clothes in which they had been captured were torn from their shoulders by the underbrush; they made the rest of their awful journey as naked as the Indians themselves.

After many days of such anguish, the Indians began to make frequent halts, at which some child would drop out of line to be turned over to a woman in an Indian village they had reached. Their captors were complying with the tribal rule that where parents had lost any of their children in warfare they must be recompensed with captives, henceforth their slaves, with adoption into the tribe as their sole hope of mitigating the misery of their lot.

"Barbara," whispered Regina to her sister, "will they leave one of us in one place and carry the other further on?"

"I'm afraid so," Barbara replied.

"Oh, I don't know what I shall do if I am left all alone!" The younger sister began to cry.

"I don't know either," said Barbara. "I only hope they send thee away first. Thou wilt then be so much the nearer home. Maybe thou canst escape sometime, when thou art older."

Regina shuddered.

"I can never escape," she wept. "We are so far away now that I couldn't go back if they sent me."

Still the sisters were driven onward, in company with the slowly diminishing line of captives. It was not until many days more—naked, barefoot, laden each with her appointed burden of younger childhood—that the fateful halt came at the village which was to claim one of them. There was no warning, no preparation. Regina was shoved, the child strapped to her back, into the hut of an ill-favored old hag, of whose children only one son, a notorious village loafer, survived.

"Barbara!" she screamed in her despair.

She heard her sister's voice call a hopeless farewell, on her back the two-year-old child she had carried the distance of four hundred miles, as she was driven westward beyond her vision. The older girl bore the murderous fatigues of that journey for another one hundred miles before she found her place of slavery in the territory now comprised within the sovereign state of Ohio.

For three and a half years Barbara Leininger served her Indian mistress there as a slave, her one solace the friendship of a girl captive near her age, Maria Le Roy.

The girls gradually were given some slight measure of freedom for their owners deemed it out of all likelihood that anyone, man or woman, should ever dare the risk of flight, with so terrible a journey to follow before they could reach the English outpost. Yet, when the two young girls were just budding into womanhood, and were liable to be forced into union with some young men of the tribe, that daring venture was agreed upon by Barbara with a young Englishman, David Breckenridge, who had attained manhood in captivity. She told Maria Le Roy. The season was February, and Maria, saying she was willing enough to risk it, advised that they wait until the weather should be more mild.

But, their resolve once taken, it was hard for any of the captives to endure their wretched situation. The lapse of a month found them eager to take whatever desperate changes the close of the winter offered, and another Englishman, Owen Gibson, was enlisted in the enterprise. At ten o'clock in the night of March 16, 1759, Owen, with the noiseless tread he had learned among the Indians, reached Barbara's little lean-to and gave her the faint signal for which she waited. David had in the meantime met Maria Le Roy, and the four made their way stealthily through the quiet village, in no dread of their masters, but in deadly fear of the sixteen dogs that lurked in the lee of the huts. By some blessed mercy of providence, not a cur barked.

The flight of the group, of course, was eastward, and their speed was the greatest they could make. After some traveling, breathless for the most part, they found themselves on the bank of the Muskingum River, too bitterly cold, too wide, and too deep to ford or swim.

When Barbara Leininger and her companions, hearkening for sounds of pursuit, stood on that fateful shore, their faces toward the land that meant life and happiness, they believed that God was there beside them and would answer their appeal if they would have faith in Him. Barbara, her face wearing the rapt expression of one inspired, called upon her memories of the hymns her mother sang, mingling into one softly intoned prayer the lines that might tell their God of the dire need they suffered.

As she finished, it seemed to all of them that the prayer must have been answered from on high. They discovered a raft, fashioned by Indians and abandoned to the waters after it had served its purpose of ferriage across the Muskingum.

The current carried them a mile downstream before they could effect their landing on the opposite bank; but they were only too grateful both for their passage across that first daunting obstacle and for having put out of their pursuers' reach the one raft which could have facilitated the pursuit.

All that night and all the next day they ran until utterly exhausted, then they flung themselves on the cold ground without daring to kindle even the smallest campfire.

In the morning they awoke ravenous, and Owen was forced to risk on a bear the noise of a gunshot from the weapon he carried. The bear fell, and he ran to tomahawk it. But the bear, as the young Englishman closed in, caught his foot in his powerful jaws, inflicting three wounds which seriously lamed him, and then made its escape among the rocks. They then limped on their dangerous way, drawn with hunger pangs.

Another day passed, and still no game. But on the third day Owen killed a deer, and the roasted hindquarters refreshed the whole party. Next morning another deer, falling to the same true aim, furnished food that carried them to the Ohio River, which they reached at night, having made a detour of one hundred miles to find it.

They slept until midnight. David and Owen rose then, and built a raft on which the little party crossed. Learned enough in Indian lore to read the symbols, they found markings there which informed them that 150 miles still separated them from Fort Duquesne. But how the trail lay they could not surmise.

So they agreed that their only course was to travel straight onward toward the sunrise, and for seven days they harked back through the wilderness until they reached Little Beaver Creek, fifty miles from Pittsburgh.

It seemed as though every misfortune they had successfully weathered must befall them almost within touch of safety. Barbara, slipping into the stream, nearly drowned. Owen lost his flint and steel, and amid rain and snow, they passed four days and nights without a glimmer of fire. When, on the last day of that eventful March, they came to the river, three miles below Pittsburgh, and pushed off on a raft they had hastily flung together, it proved too small for their combined weight and began to sink under them. Maria Le Roy fell into the river and was saved only by the devotion of her companions. They returned to the bank, then the young men ferried them across the Monongahela one at a time.

Safe now, but unable in the dark to risk the frail craft in reaching the fort beyond, they called for aid. Colonel Hugh Mercer, in command, sent a boat; but the men in it, for a time believing the strangers were Indians, refused to take them in. It was almost impossible to persuade the soldiers that the two girls with their companions had made the appalling journey from the far land of the savages. But at length, when the shivering fugitives adduced fact after fact in support of their declaration, the boat's crew consented to forego the evidence of their eyes, took them aboard, and speedily landed them at the fort.

Once there, and the salient features of their story known, they were given every help and comfort. Colonel Mercer ordered each of the girls provided with a new chemise, a petticoat, stockings, garters, and such other items as decency and warmth demanded. A day later he sent them forward under guard of a detachment of soldiers commanded by Lieutenant Samuel Miles, to Fort Ligonier, where the lieutenant presented them with blankets. On April 15, under the protection of Captain Philip Weiser and Lieutenant Samuel J. Atlee, they were escorted to Fort Bedford, where they remained for a week. They found accommodation in wagons as far as Harris Ferry and thence, afoot, they took their way to Lancaster and on to Philadelphia, where they were reunited with their families.

———————

Meanwhile, through all those years, Barbara's young sister, Regina, had lived the true slave's life in the service of the hag to whom her captors had given her. The younger girl's evil augury that, though she might be nearer the settlements than her sister, she could never escape was destined to be correct.

The old squaw's son was the true type of young Indian loafer and sport. He went away for days and weeks at a time and, for all he cared, left his mother to starve.

Regina, in her lowly status of slave girl, was given the alternative of providing food for the squalid household or of being put to death.

Naked, starving, the child gathered the wood that supplied warmth for the miserable shack of boughs in which they huddled. She dug in the fields and woods for roots, artichokes, garlic, and whatever might prove edible, not excepting the bark of some trees. When the ground froze, she hunted like a wild beast for field mice, wood rats, and other small animals that could stay the pangs of hunger.

As the years went by, the child she had carried into the village on her back grew big enough to be of some help in that desperate, unremitting struggle against starvation. Regina herself, her youthful vitality responding to the hardships of her existence, developed into magnificent young womanhood, tall and strong of frame, her body bronzed under the sunlight, her regular features making her a rarely beautiful Indian maiden.

Outwardly, she appeared reconciled to her fate. She spoke the tribal language, she lived the tribal life; from her memory the recollection of even her mother's face departed.

But in her heart she treasured her native tongue; and above all, she cherished the words of the hymns in which, in the cabin home on the cruel border line, she had joined her childish treble to the strong inspiring volume of her mother's notes.

When she found herself alone with her young companion in the forest, drudging at the task of reaping where no one had sowed, Regina would kneel, and her heart welling with fond, unavailing memories, repeat the words of those hymns solemnly as her prayers for deliverance. As she neared womanhood there began to dawn in her soul a simple, trusting faith that some time in some way, how she knew not, the hour of her release from bondage must arrive.

She was almost nineteen years old when the bold campaign against the tribes pushed by Colonel Bouquet into their remotest fortresses beyond the Ohio, compelled the savages to sue for peace.

"The first condition under which any mercy can be shown," he notified the beaten chiefs, "must be the immediate surrender into my keeping of every white prisoner held captive in every village of your tribes."

It was a strange and often shocking spectacle that followed, during the ensuing weeks, there in the trackless wilderness, while the victorious whites received from the savages hundreds of their race—men, women, and children—who had been mourned as dead or as forever lost by the few kin surviving the successive massacres.

In the midst of winter the poor creatures came, singly and in groups, well nigh naked. The officers and the soldiers vied with one another in sacrificing portions of their uniforms, which could be used to supply some few of their charges with covering. As swiftly as marches could be made they conveyed the wretched throng to Fort Pitt. The garrison there emulated the men returning from the field. They gave up their capes, sleeves, pocket flaps, pockets, collars, unneeded portions of their shirts, their cravats, extra blanket lengths—every smallest scrap of material which could be fashioned into extra clothing; and then, officers and men, they turned cutters and seamstresses and made the garments.

Word was now sent forward throughout Pennsylvania that the army of the rescued would be brought as far as Carlisle, where members of any family who had lost dear ones could come and claim their own, and the march to Carlisle followed.

History may afford no parallel for the mingling of the dramatic with the tragic which developed in the thrilling scene enacted in Carlisle on December 31, 1764, before English commissioners appointed to supervise the restoration of the captives to their families. All the prisoners of the Indians had not been spared to slavery as children. The varied fortunes of the recurring wars and raids had led the savages to carry off wives and husbands, as well as daughters and sons.

And there, on one hand an immense throng of whites, young and old, confronted a great crowd of brown-skinned people, who, where they were dressed at all, wore Joseph's coat of many colors or the wild scant garments of the Indians with whom they had to live so long. There were husbands who recognized instantly wives ravished from their homes, there were parents who could not recognize their own children. Laughter and tears, the extremes of joy and heartbreaking despair, met side by side amid those reunions and those failures of loved ones to find their own.

The journey to the grist mill on the cruel morning of the Penn's Creek massacre had saved Mrs. Leininger and her older boy from the fate of her younger son and her husband. She came to Carlisle, a woman changed and aged in her nine long years of grief, hoping passionately that her daughter Regina would be among the captives.

But now she stood, heart-wrung and sad-eyed, turning to the commissioners to implore their aid in identifying her. She told them, with a mother's fond words, of the Regina she had loved, the little girl of ten, so good and so gentle, whose pleasure was the singing of their homely German hymns.

"Do you remember the words of one of those hymns?" suddenly inquired a grave member of the official group.

"Ach, surely! She loved most the hymn 'Alone, Yet Not Alone Am I,' and 'Jesus, Evermore I Love.'"

"Why, then, step forth and sing it. It may be the child, no doubt a woman grown by this time, will recognize words or voice." Those nearest them noted, idly at the moment—for their own affairs were engrossing—a matron walking a few steps forward, where she might be free of the press of embraces and rejoicing surrounding her anguished suspense. Then, above the tumult, her face aglow with the longing of her mother love, and looking straight at the quivering group of captives still unclaimed, the mother of Regina Leininger raised her voice in the beautiful words of that old, sweet hymn of unfaltering faith:

> Alone, yet not alone am I
> Though in this solitude so dread—

From the bronzed mass of humanity before her a tall, powerful girl, known only by her Indian name, Sawquehanna—the White Lily—sprang and ran forward. As she ran she sang:

> I feel my Saviour always nigh;
> He comes the weary hours to cheer

The mother's voice went on; in it there sounded a new note of sublime happiness, which, for once, took from their own joys and griefs the hearts of the hundreds who heard and saw; and although both felt at once that they were mother and child, their deep inbred religious sentiment so filled them with gratitude to the Most High that they stood, their arms outstretched in eagerness, yet waiting to clasp each other in an embrace until they finished the stanza together:

> I am with Him and He with me,
> E'en here alone I cannot be.

Then the mother, her graying head in silent prayer, drew to her bosom the child she had mourned so long.

"Ach, mutter, mutter!" cried Regina. "I remember them all. Listen! I must prove to thee again that I am thy little Regina."

She sang the rest of the hymn, and "Jesus, Evermore I Love." But as she began the second hymn, a brown little girl just growing into her teens ran from among the captives, and, catching her hand, joined in the words. When Regina, immediately afterward, recited the Apostles' Creed, the child repeated with her the solemn declaration of faith. She was the baby Regina had carried on her back into the hut of the old hag they were given to.

No one ever claimed the girl; but she, with every clinging tenderness of her child nature, claimed Regina. And so the mother, who had come, hoping she might recover one daughter, returned to her home with two.

HENRY MELCHIOR MUHLENBERG (1711–1787) *was born in Einbeck, Hanover. After studying at the Universities of Göttingen and Halle, he immigrated to America in 1742. He is generally considered to be the father of America's Lutheran churches, organizing the first Lutheran synod in 1748.*

THE DEATH DISK

Mark Twain

A life was at stake on the little girl's choice. Her *father's*. Would she make the right choice? The story is based on an actual event, chronicled by Thomas Carlyle in his *Letters and Speeches of Oliver Cromwell*—Cromwell, the only ruler not a monarch that England has ever had.

More perhaps than any other story he ever wrote, this story reveals Twain's soft side, his love for children.

This was Oliver Cromwell's time. Colonel Mayfair was the youngest officer of his rank in the armies of the Commonwealth, he being but thirty years old. But young as he was, he was a veteran soldier, and tanned and war-worn, for he had begun his military life at seventeen; he had fought in many battles, and had won his high place in the service and in the admiration of men, step by step, by valor in the field. But he was in deep trouble now; a shadow had fallen upon his fortunes.

The winter evening was come, and outside were storm and darkness; within, a melancholy silence; for the Colonel and his young wife had talked their sorrow out, had read the evening chapter and prayed the evening prayer, and there was nothing more to do but sit hand in hand and gaze into the fire and think—and wait. They would not have to wait long; they knew that, and the wife shuddered at the thought.

They had one child: Abby, seven years old, their idol. She would come presently for a good-night kiss, and the Colonel spoke now, and said: "Dry away the tears and let us seem happy, for her sake. We must forget, for the time, that which is to happen."

"I will. I will shut them up in my heart, which is breaking."

"And we will accept what is appointed for us, and bear it in patience, as knowing that whatsoever He doeth is done in righteousness and meant in kindness—"

"Saying, 'His will be done.' Yes, I can say it with all my mind and soul. I wish I could say it with my heart. Oh, if I could! If this dear hand which I press and kiss for the last time—"

"Sh! Sweetheart, she is coming!"

A curly-headed little figure in nightclothes glided in at the door and ran to the father, and was gathered to his breast and fervently kissed once, twice, three times.

"Why, Papa, you mustn't kiss me like that: you rumple my hair."

"Oh, I am so sorry—so sorry. Do you forgive me, dear?"

"Why, of course, Papa. But *are* you sorry? Not pretending, but real, right down sorry?"

"Well, you can judge for yourself, Abby," and he covered his face with his hands and pretended to sob. The child was filled with remorse to see this tragic thing which she had caused, and she began to cry herself, and to tug at the hands, and say:

"Oh, don't, Papa, please don't cry; Abby didn't mean it; Abby

John Milton playing for Oliver Cromwell and his family

wouldn't ever do it again. Please, Papa!" Tugging and straining to separate the fingers, she got a fleeting glimpse of an eye behind them, and cried out: "Why, you naughty Papa, you're not crying at all! You're only fooling! And Abby is going to Mamma, now: you don't treat Abby right."

She was all for climbing down, but her father wound his arms about her and said: "No, stay with me, dear: Papa *was* naughty, and confesses it, and is sorry—there, let him kiss the tears away—and he begs Abby's forgiveness, and will do anything Abby says he must do, for a punishment; they're all kissed away now, and not a curl rumpled—and whatever Abby commands—"

And so it was made up, and all in a moment the sunshine was

back again and burning brightly in the child's face, and she was patting her father's cheeks and naming the penalty: "A story! A story!"

Hark!

The elders stopped breathing, and listened. Footsteps! faintly caught between the gusts of wind. They came nearer—louder, louder—then passed by and faded away. The elders drew deep breaths of relief, and the papa said: "A story, is it? A happy one?"

"No, Papa: a dreadful one."

Papa wanted to shift to the happy kind, but the child stood by her rights. As per agreement, she was to have anything she commanded. He was a good Puritan soldier and had passed his word. He saw that he must make it good. She explained her reason:

"Papa, we mustn't always have gay ones. Nurse says people don't always have gay times. Is that true, Papa? She *says* so."

The mama sighed, and her thoughts drifted to her troubles again. The papa said, gently: "It's true, dear. Troubles have to come; it's a pity, but it's true."

"Oh, then tell a story about them, Papa—a dreadful one, so that we'll shiver, and feel just as if it was *us*. Mamma, you snuggle up close, and hold one of Abby's hands, so that if it's too dreadful it'll be easier for us to bear it if we're all snuggled up together, you know. Now you can begin, Papa."

"Well, once there were three colonels—"

"Oh, goody! *I* know colonels, just as easy! It's because you are one, and I know the clothes. Go on, Papa."

"And in a battle they had committed a breach of discipline."

The large words struck the child's ear pleasantly, and she looked up, full of wonder and interest, and said:

"Is it something good to eat, Papa?"

The parents almost smiled, and the father answered:

"No, quite another matter, dear. They exceeded their orders."

"Is *that* someth—"

"No; it's as uneatable as the other. They were ordered to feign an attack on a strong position in a losing fight, in order to draw the enemy about and give the Commonwealth's forces a chance to retreat; but in their enthusiasm they overstepped their orders, for they turned the feint into a fact, and carried the position by storm, and won the day and the battle. The Lord General was very angry at their disobedience, and praised them highly, and ordered them to London to be tried for their lives."

"Is it the great General Cromwell, Papa?"

"Yes."

"Oh, I've seen *him*, Papa! and when he goes by our house so grand on his big horse, with the soldiers, he looks so—so—well, I don't know just how, only he looks as if he isn't satisfied, and you can see the people are afraid of him; but *I'm* not afraid of him, because he didn't look like that at me."

"Oh, you dear prattler! Well, the colonels came prisoners to London, and were put upon their honor, and allowed to go and see their families for the last—"

Hark!

They listened. Footsteps again; but again they passed by. The mamma leaned her head upon her husband's shoulder to hide her paleness.

"They arrived this morning."

The child's eyes opened wide.

"Why, Papa! Is it a *true* story?"

"Yes, dear."

"Oh, how good! Oh, it's ever so much better! Go on, Papa. Why, Mamma! *Dear* Mamma, are you crying?"

"Never mind me, dear. I was thinking of the—of the—the poor families."

"But *don't* cry, Mamma: it'll all come out right—you'll see; stories always do. Go on, Papa, to where they lived happy ever after; then she won't cry any more. You'll see, Mamma. Go on, Papa."

"First, they took them to the Tower before they let them go home."

"Oh, *I* know the Tower! We can see it from here. Go on, Papa."

"I *am* going on as well as I can, in the circumstances. In the Tower the military court tried them for an hour, and found them guilty, and condemned them to be shot."

"*Killed,* Papa?"

"Yes."

"Oh, how naughty! *Dear* Mamma, you're crying again. Don't, Mamma; it'll soon come to the good place—you'll see. Hurry, Papa, for Mamma's sake; you don't go fast enough."

"I know I don't, but I suppose it's because I stop so much to reflect."

"But you mustn't *do* it, Papa; you must go right on."

"Very well, then. The three colonels—"

"Do you know them, Papa?"

"Yes, dear."

"Oh, I wish *I* did! I love colonels. Would they let me kiss them, do you think?" The colonel's voice was a little unsteady when he answered:

"*One* of them would, my darling! There—kiss me for him."

"There, Papa—and these two are for the others. I think they would let me kiss them, Papa; for I would say, 'My papa is a colonel, too, and brave, and he would do what you did; so it *can't* be wrong, no matter what those people say, and you needn't be the least bit ashamed'; then they would let me—wouldn't they, Papa?"

"God knows they would, child!"

"Mamma! Oh, Mamma, you mustn't. He's soon coming to the happy place; go on, Papa."

"Then, some were sorry—they all were; that military court, I mean; and they went to the Lord General, and said they'd done their duty—for it *was* their duty, you know—and now they begged that two of the colonels might be spared, and only the other one shot. One would be sufficient for an example for the army, they thought. But the Lord General was very stern, and rebuked them forasmuch as, having done *their* duty and cleared their consciences, they would beguile him to do less, and so smirch his soldierly honor. But they answered that they were asking nothing of him that they wouldn't do themselves if they stood in his great place and held in their hands the noble prerogative of mercy. That struck him, and he paused and stood thinking, some of the sternness passing out of his face. Presently he bid them wait, and he retired to seek counsel of God in prayer; and when he came again, he said: 'They shall cast lots. That shall decide it, and two of them shall live.'"

"And did they Papa, did they? And which one is to die? Ah, that poor man!"

"No. They refused."

"They wouldn't do it, Papa?"

"No."

"Why?"

"They said that the one that got the fatal bean would be sentencing himself to death by his own voluntary act, and it would be but suicide, call it by what name one might. They said they were Christians, and the Bible forbade men to take their own lives. They sent back that word, and said they were ready—let the court's sentence be carried into effect."

"What does that mean, Papa?"

"They—they will all be shot."

Hark!

The wind? No. Tramp, tramp, tramp, r-r-r-umble-dumdum, r-r-r-rumble-dumdum....

"Open—in the Lord General's name!"

"Oh, goody, Papa, it's the soldiers! I love the soldiers! Let *me* let them in, Papa, let *me!*"

She jumped down, and scampered to the door and pulled it open, crying joyously: "Come in! Come in! Here they are, Papa! Grenadiers! *I* know the Grenadiers!"

The file marched in and straightened up in line at shoulder arms; its officer saluted, the doomed colonel standing erect and returning the courtesy, the soldier wife standing at his side, white, and with features drawn with inward pain, but giving no other sign of her misery, the child gazing on the show with dancing eyes....

One long embrace, of father, mother, and child; then the order, "To the Tower! Forward!" Then the colonel marched forth from the house with military step and bearing, the file following; then the door closed.

"Oh, Mamma, didn't it come out beautiful! I *told* you it would; and they're going to the Tower, and he'll *see* them! He—"

"Oh, come to my arms, you poor innocent thing!"

The next morning the stricken mother was not able to leave her bed; doctors and nurses were watching by her, and whispering together now and then; Abby could not be allowed in the room; she was told to run and play; Mamma was very ill. The child, muffled in winter wraps, went out and played in the street awhile; then it struck her as strange, and also wrong, that her papa should be allowed to stay at the Tower in ignorance at such a time as this. This must be remedied: she would attend to it in person.

An hour later the military court were ushered into the presence of the Lord General. He stood grim and erect, with his knuckles resting upon the table, and indicated that he was ready to listen. The spokesman said: "We have urged them to reconsider; we have implored them: but they persist. They will not cast lots. They are willing to die, but not to violate their religion."

The Protector's face darkened, but he said nothing. He remained a time in thought, then he said: "They shall not all die; the lots shall be cast *for* them." Gratitude shown in the faces of the court. "Send for them. Place them in that room there. Stand them side by side with their faces to the wall and their wrists crossed behind them. Let me know when they are there."

When he was alone he sat down, and presently gave this order to an attendant: "Go, bring me the first little child that passes by."

The man was hardly out at the door before he was back again, leading Abby by the hand, her garments lightly powdered with snow. She went straight to the Head of the State, that formidable personage at the mention of whose name the principalities and powers of the earth trembled, and climbed up in his lap, and said:

"I know *you*, sir: you are the Lord General; I've seen you; I've seen you when you went by my house. Everybody was afraid; but *I* wasn't afraid, because you didn't look cross at *me;* you remember, don't you? I had on my red frock—the one with the blue things on it down the front. Don't you remember that?"

A smile softened the austere lines of the Protector's face, and he began to struggle diplomatically with his answer:

"Why, let me see—I—"

"I was standing right by the house—*my* house, you know."

"Well, you dear little thing, I ought to be ashamed, but you know—"

The child interrupted, reproachfully.

"Now you *don't* remember it. Why, I didn't forget *you*."

"Now I *am* ashamed: but I will never forget you again, dear; you have my word for it. You'll forgive me now, won't you, and be good friends with me, always and forever?"

"Yes, indeed I will, though I don't know how you came to forget it; you must be very forgetful: but I am too, sometimes. I can forgive you without any trouble, for I think you *mean* to be good and do right, and I think you're just as kind. But you must snuggle me better, the way Papa does—it's cold."

"You shall be snuggled to your heart's content, little new friend of mine, always to be *old* friend of mine hereafter, isn't it? You remind me of my little girl—not little any more, now—but she was dear, and sweet, and daintily made, like you. And she had your charm, your all-conquering sweet confidence in friend and stranger alike, that wins to willing slavery any upon whom its precious compliment falls. She used to lie in my arms, just as you're doing now; and charm the weariness and care out of my heart and give it peace, just as you're doing now; and we were comrades, and equals, and playfellows together. Ages ago it was, since that pleasant heaven faded away and vanished, and you've brought it back again; take a burdened man's blessing for it, you tiny creature, who are carrying the weight of England while I rest!"

"Did you love her very, very, *very* much?"

"Ah, you shall judge by this: she commanded and I obeyed!"

"I think you are lovely! Will you kiss me?"

"Thankfully, and hold it a privilege, too. There—this one is for you; and there—this one is for her. You made it a request; and you could have made it a command, for you are representing her, and what you command I must obey."

The child clapped her hands with delight at the idea of this grand promotion, then her ear caught an approaching sound: the measured tramp of marching men.

"Soldiers! Soldiers, Lord General! Abby wants to see them!"

You shall, dear; but wait a moment, I have a commission for you."

An officer entered and bowed low, saying, "They are come, your Highness," bowed again, and retired.

The Head of the Nation gave Abby three little disks of sealing-wax: two white, and one a ruddy red, for this one's mission was to deliver death to the colonel who should get it.

"Oh, what a lovely red one! Are they for me?"

"No, dear; they are for others. Lift the corner of that curtain, there, which hides an open door; pass through, and you'll see three men standing in a row, with their backs toward you and their hands behind their backs—so—each with one hand open, like a cup. Into each of the open hands drop one of those things, then come back to me."

Abby disappeared behind the curtain, and the Protector was alone. He said, reverently: "Of a surety that good thought came to me in my perplexity from Him who is an ever-present help to them that are in doubt and seek His aid. He knoweth where the choice should fall, and has sent His sinless messenger to do His will. Another would err, but He cannot err. Wonderful are His ways, and wise—blessed be His holy name!"

The small fairy dropped the curtain behind her and stood for a moment studying with alert curiosity the appointments of the chamber of doom, and the rigid figures of the soldiery and the prisoners; then her face lighted merrily, and she said to herself: *why,*

one of them is Papa! I know his back. He shall have the prettiest one!
She tripped gaily forward and dropped the disks into the open
hands, then peeped around under her father's arm, and lifted her
laughing face and cried out:

"Papa! Papa! Look what you've got. *I* gave it to you!"

He glanced at the fatal gift, then sank to his knees and gathered
his innocent little executioner to his breast in an agony of love and
pity. Soldiers, officers, released prisoners, all stood paralyzed, for a
moment, at the vastness of this tragedy, then the pitiful scene
smote their hearts, their eyes filled, and they wept unashamed.
There was deep and reverent silence during some minutes, then the
officer of the guard moved reluctantly forward and touched his
prisoner on the shoulder, saying, gently:

"It grieves me, sir, but my duty commands."

"Commands what?" said the child.

"I must take him away. I am so sorry."

"Take him away? *Where?*"

"To—to—God help me!—to another part of the fortress."

"Indeed you can't. My mamma is sick, and I'm going to take
him home." She released herself and climbed upon her father's
back and put her arms around his neck. "Now Abby's ready, Papa.
Come along."

"My poor child, I can't. I must go with them."

The child jumped to the ground and looked about her, wondering. Then she ran and stood before the officer and stamped her
small foot indignantly and cried out:

"I told you my mamma is sick, and you might have listened.
Let him go. You *must!*"

"Oh, poor child, would God I could, but indeed I must take
him away. Attention, guard! Fall in! Shoulder arms!"

Abby was gone like a flash of light. In a moment she was back, dragging the Lord Protector by the hand. At this formidable apparition all present straightened up, the officers saluting and the soldiers presenting arms.

"Stop them, sir! My mamma is sick and wants my papa, and I *told* them so, but they never listened to me, and are taking him away."

The Lord General stood as one dazed.

"*Your* papa, child? Is he your papa?"

"Why, of course. He was *always* it. Would I give the pretty red one to any other, when I love him so? No!"

A shocked expression rose in the Protector's face, and he said:

"Ah, God help me! Through Satan's wiles I have done the cruelest thing that ever man did, and there is no help, no help! What can I do?"

Abby cried out, distressed and impatient: "Why you can make them let him go," and she began to sob. "Tell them to do it! You told me to command, and now the very first time I tell you to do a thing you don't do it!"

A tender light dawned in the rugged old face, and the Lord General laid his hand upon the small tyrant's head and said: "God be thanked for the saving accident of that unthinking promise; and you, inspired by Him, for reminding me of my forgotten pledge, O incomparable child! Officer, obey her command—she speaks by my mouth. The prisoner is pardoned; set him free!"

MARK TWAIN, *pseudonym of Samuel Langhorne Clemens (1835–1910) grew up in Hannibal, Missouri. Twain is generally considered one of the giants of American literature, writing many short stories as well as classics such as* Tom Sawyer, Life on the Mississippi, Innocents Abroad, *and* Huckleberry Finn.

Two Candles
for St. Anthony

Arthur Milward

He came to think of Jeremy as a three-layer cake—angelic, street-wise, and lovable. But Jeremy was also a friend to lovely little Stephanie. And both of them were confronted by tragedy. Where was he to turn?

His blue eyes, long, curling lashes, and fair skin made him look almost like a choirboy. That, however, was just an initial impression. Eleven-year-old Jeremy may or may not have sung in the choir of the church which he attended—if, indeed, he did attend a church—but he was certainly no angel. His innocent, ingenuous appearance left one unprepared for the tough little Cockney behind those clear, blue eyes.

Yet I quickly realized as I came to know him that there was a good deal more to Jeremy than met the eye. With increasing frequency, after a typically wary appraisal, he would perch himself on my little son's bed across from his own in the terminal ward of the

Children's Hospital as Ady was dropping off to sleep early in the evening and, after my little boy was safely asleep, would engage me in earnest conversation. I suppose it could be called conversation. Actually, Jeremy talked and I listened.

I came to think of him as a sort of attractively assembled three-layer cake: the angelic-appearing exterior disguising a tough, street-wise Cockney child, wise, in some ways, far beyond his years, and deeper still, a kind and affectionate little boy.

We—at least, he—talked about many things, but most often about the other occupants of the ward. As long as they respected his "territorial rights," Jeremy got on well with the other child patients, whose ages ranged from around four years old to the twelve-year-old "senior citizens." Some, though, understandably, he liked better than others.

He especially liked Stephanie—but then it was impossible not to like Stephanie. Ten years old, she was—even now, with a shaven head and disfigured with sundry tubes and other protuberances and painfully thin—an unusually pretty—no, beautiful child. She, too, had cornflower-blue eyes and it was still possible to see that her hair had been like golden silk. It used to hang down to her waist, her mother told us—Jeremy and me—a bit tearfully, and showed us a picture to prove it.

Stephanie was an unusual child. Perhaps because of her long—and losing—battle with a malignancy, she was at once quite child-like and yet old for her age. Her temperament—which matched her appearance—endeared her to everyone. Unfailingly polite, she never became impatient or querulous, even when her discomfort became acute. Always appreciative of any small service performed for her comfort, she smiled frequently—albeit sometimes through tears.

Jeremy quite quickly appointed himself guardian-cum-body

servant for Stephanie. Unlike the little girl, he was, for the most part, ambulatory, and he waited upon her untiringly, fetching and carrying, fixing her pillows, and generally doing whatever he could to lessen her inevitable discomfort.

Sometimes he would draw up a chair and just sit by her bed, not saying anything, holding her hand in his own, until she drifted off to sleep. No one said anything to him about his evident affection for the little girl. Even the youngest among us recognized that it wasn't the sort of situation to provide an opportunity for teasing. The other children realized, too, that if anyone had been inclined to make what he felt to be an uncalled-for comment, Jeremy was quite capable of taking immediate and violent action.

Perhaps as a result, to some extent, of our one-sided "conversations," Jeremy and I came to understand one another quite well over the period of some months when we saw each other almost daily. So when I chanced to look across at him one evening as I sat by Ady's bed watching him drop off to sleep, I was not really surprised to see the tears on Jeremy's face as he sat beside Stephanie's bed holding the little girl's hand as she hovered between waking and sleeping. He saw me looking at him but didn't turn away. He merely smiled faintly as he leaned over and wiped her damp forehead with a tissue he held in his hand.

Cherubic appearance notwithstanding, I didn't regard Jeremy as a religious child, but I came to realize that the inside of a church was not totally unfamiliar to him. I knew he was—nominally at least—a Catholic, because of the rosary hanging over his bed, although I never saw him actually using it. I only knew him to "go to church" once during the period of our acquaintance.

One member of the staff of remarkably compassionate and dedicated nurses who cared for the "terminal" children made it a regular practice—on her days off duty—to stop by the ward and escort those of the children who were able to accompany her to a nearby park for an hour's play and change of scenery. Occasionally, if this activity coincided with my visit, I would go along and help push the children on the swings or join them in feeding the ducks on the park pond with bread brought from the ward kitchen for the purpose.

Jeremy wouldn't always go along with the expedition. Often he would stay behind to keep Stephanie company in the absence of the other children. If she was asleep or temporarily elsewhere for treatment, however, he would come along and never failed to return with a bunch of flowers he had "appropriated" from one of the park flower beds.

One morning, however, after Stephanie had finally drifted off to sleep, exhausted after a particularly bad night of constantly recurring seizures and much pain, Jeremy accompanied the "park contingent" to the iron gates of the park and, as we were about to enter, beckoned to the nurse and whispered something in her ear. Upon receiving what was evidently her approval, he trotted off down the street and disappeared into the Catholic church about a block away. The nurse called me back from the group of excited children who were impatiently propelling me toward the duck pond and asked me if I would mind dropping by the church to keep an eye on Jeremy and escort him back to the group in due course.

In a matter of moments I found myself in the unaccustomed surroundings of the church. Though Protestant by heredity and persuasion, I have long been of the opinion that our common Father does not confine Himself to any one creed, place, or practice, but is available to us whenever and wherever we seek Him.

As my eyes accustomed themselves to the dimness of the church's interior, I saw that Jeremy and I appeared to be the sole occupants of the building. Jeremy was evidently unaware of my presence, and I drew back into the shadows, unwilling to intrude on his privacy.

Taking some coins from his pocket, the boy dropped them into the box provided, took a taper, and lit a candle which he placed in a holder before a statue of a rubicund-appearing gentleman—evidently a representation of a saint. He genuflected perfunctorily toward the high altar, dropped onto his knees before the statue, and began to plead with the one represented. I remained standing silently in the shadows.

"Please, St. Anthony," begged the boy, "ask Him to please help Stephanie. I know she's going to die, but please ask Him not to let her hurt so bad. Don't let her keep having those seizures. It hurts her so and she's frightened. She's only ten, you know, St. Anthony. She's just a kid. Please, dear St. Anthony, tell Him if He has to have somebody hurting, let me hurt instead. I don't mind. Really I don't. I know I'm going to die soon too. Tell Him, please, St. Anthony, to let me hurt instead of her. In the name of Our Lord. Amen."

I saw the tears on his face as he passed by me on his way out of the church. He didn't see me, and I made no move. I waited for a few moments, dried my own tears, and followed him to the park gates where he had rejoined the other children now congregating around the swings and seesaws. I nodded to the nurse that everything was under control, and we proceeded to take turns swinging the excited children until it was time for us to return the few blocks to the hospital.

Three days later when I made my daily visit to my little son, I noted that Stephanie's bed was occupied by a small boy. He looked to be about seven years old. He told me his name was Ronnie.

I asked no questions and nobody made any comment. It wasn't

that sort of ward. Nobody—not even the youngest—ever asked why a bed was suddenly empty or occupied by a newcomer. Everybody—even the youngest—sensed it was something that nobody could bear to talk about.

Later I looked for one of the nurses I knew. "About three o'clock this morning," she told me.

"Was it bad?" I ventured.

"I've seen worse," the nurse responded, "but yes, it was pretty bad."

I looked for Jeremy, anxious as to how he was taking the tragic turn of events. He was lying—fully dressed—on his bed, curled up into a ball, with his back toward the other occupants of the ward. Clearly, right now, Jeremy didn't feel like talking to anyone. I decided to leave well enough alone.

When I visited the ward over the following two days, Jeremy ignored me, as, indeed, he did everybody else. He spoke to no one, and if anybody approached him, he looked through them as if they weren't there. On the third evening, however, somewhat to my surprise, and, I think, to my relief, he joined me as I was about to leave the ward after watching Ady drop off to sleep. We walked into the corridor together.

He planted himself in front of me, his legs apart and his fists clenched. He looked straight at me. His eyes held fear—or hate—or despair? Possibly all three.

"I hate God," he told me, quietly but vehemently. "He's a liar and a cheat. I don't believe there is a God."

Somewhat taken aback by the child's intensity, I was at a loss for a response.

I suppose I could have pointed out the obvious inconsistency of his statements. I could have spoken to him of the "reason" for human suffering and the necessity for faith and acceptance. I did none of these things. The little boy's outburst was too close to home. I had shared dangerously similar feelings myself during the last several months. Recalling only too well where Jeremy was "coming from," I couldn't find it in my heart to rebuke him. I remained silent. I took a tentative step toward the white-faced child and took him in my arms. He was crying now. He stiffened at first, then relaxed and clung to me, sobbing.

After several minutes, he broke away and returned to the ward.

After this, Jeremy seemed to lose interest in everything. Time was running out for him. He had, it seemed, given up on life. Three weeks later, when I entered the ward and walked over to Ady's bed, I looked for Jeremy in vain.

Time was running out for my little boy, too. Several years younger than Jeremy, he firmly believed he would be healed, that Jesus would make him "all better." I tried to believe too.

Not long after this, on one of our periodic "jaunts" to the local park, I left the group momentarily and, on an impulse, ran down the street to the nearby Catholic church.

Entering the dimly lit church, I smelled the now somewhat familiar odor of incense and hot wax. Making my way over to the area where I had observed Jeremy on my previous visit, I, in turn, dropped some coins into the box, selected a candle—one of the fat, long-burning ones—knelt down in the place where Jeremy had knelt, and poured out my petition.

"Oh, God, can I change a prayer? I've been pleading with You for so long. Can I change my prayer? Oh, Father, please let him rest. Don't let him hurt any more."

Not without misgivings, I rose from my knees and returned to the children and the nurse. "Where d'ya go?" inquired seven-year-old Jamie as I rejoined the group.

"Mind your own," admonished nine-year-old Annie, frowning at him. "'E 'ad to go to the gents, o' course."

Four days later, at two o'clock in the morning, my prayer was answered.

Now, years later, I never pass a Catholic church without thinking of Jeremy—the tough little Cockney with love in his heart.

Not infrequently, I reproach myself for not taking the opportunity to talk to him about the love of God, His compassion, and the need for acceptance of His will.

At the time, however, I had no words for Jeremy. All I could do was hold him. Maybe that was enough.

ARTHUR MILWARD *was born in England and later immigrated to America. Besides his career in printing, he has a second—writing. A number of his true stories have been carried all over the world by* Reader's Digest. *Today, Mr. Milward lives and writes from Kennett Square, Pennsylvania.*

QUALITY

John Galsworthy

Quality—is it true, as Emerson submitted, that if you build a better mousetrap, the world will beat a path to your door? Or are there other forces at work—forces such as planned obsolescence?

I have read this story to my college literature students many times, and every time I get to the last line...there is *silence*.

I knew him from the days of my extreme youth, because he made my father's boots. He and his elder brother inhabited two little shops combined into one in a small bystreet—now no more, but then most fashionably placed in the West End. That tenement had a certain quiet distinction; there was no sign upon its face that he made for any of the Royal Family—merely his own German name of Gessler Brothers, and in the window a few pairs of boots. I remember that it always troubled me to account for those unvarying boots in the window, for he made only what was ordered, reaching nothing down, and it seemed so inconceivable that what he made could ever have failed to fit. Had he bought them to put there? That, too, seemed inconceivable. He would never have tolerated in the house, leather on which he had not worked himself. Besides, they were too beautiful—the pair of pumps, so inexpressibly slim, the patent leathers with cloth tops, making water come into one's mouth, the tall brown riding boots with marvelous sooty glow, as if, though new, they had been worn a hundred years. Those pairs could only have been made by one who saw before him the Soul of Boot—so truly were they prototypes incarnating the very spirit of all footgear. These thoughts, of course, came to me later, though even when I was promoted to him, at the age of perhaps fourteen, some inkling haunted me of the dignity of himself and brother. For to make boots—such boots as he made—seemed to me then, and still seems to me, mysterious and wonderful.

I remember well my shy remark, one day, while stretching out to him my youthful foot:

"Isn't it awfully hard to do, Mr. Gessler?"

And his answer, given with a sudden smile from out of the sardonic redness of his beard: "Id is an Ardt!"

Himself, he was a little as if made from leather, with his yellow crinkly face, and crinkly reddish hair and beard, and neat folds slanting down his cheeks to the corners of his mouth, and his guttural and one-toned voice, for leather is a sardonic substance, and stiff and slow of purpose. And that was the character of his face, save that his eyes, which were gray-blue, had in them the simple gravity of one secretly possessed by the Ideal. His elder brother was so very like him—though watery, paler in every way, with a great industry—that sometimes in early days I was not quite sure of him until the interview was over. Then I knew that it was he, if the words, "I will ask my brudder," had not been spoken; and that, if they had, it was his elder brother.

When one grew old and wild and ran up bills, one somehow

never ran them up with Gessler Brothers. It would not have seemed becoming to go in there and stretch out one's foot to that blue iron-spectacled glance, owing him for more than—say—two pairs, just the comfortable reassurance that one was still his client.

For it was not possible to go to him very often—his boots lasted terribly, having something beyond the temporary—some, as it were, essence of boot stitched into them.

One went in, not as into most shops, in the mood of: "Please serve me, and let me go!" but restfully, as one enters a church; and, sitting on the single wooden chair, waited—for there was never anybody there. Soon, over the top edge of that sort of well—rather dark, and smelling soothingly of leather—which formed the shop, there would be seen his face, or that of his elder brother, peering down. A guttural sound, and the tip-tap of bast slippers beating the narrow wooden stairs, and he would stand before one without coat, a little bent, in leather apron, with sleeves turned back, blinking—as if awakened from some dream of boots, or like an owl surprised in daylight and annoyed at this interruption.

And I would say: "How do you do, Mr. Gessler? Could you make me a pair of Russia leather boots?"

Without a word he would leave me, retiring whence he came, or into the other portion of the shop, and I would continue to rest in the wooden chair, inhaling the incense of his trade. Soon he would come back, holding in his thin, veined hand a piece of gold-brown leather. With eyes fixed on it, he would remark: "What a beautiful biece!" When I, too, had admired it, he would speak again. "When do you wand dem?" And I would answer: "Oh! As soon as you conveniently can." And he would say: "Tomorrow fordnightd?" Or if he were his elder brother: "I will ask my brudder!"

Then I would murmur: "Thank you! Good morning, Mr.

Gessler." "Goot morning!" he would reply, still looking at the leather in his hand. And as I moved to the door, I would hear the tip-tap of his bast slippers restoring him, up the stairs, to his dream of boots. But if it were some new kind of footgear that he had not yet made me, then indeed he would observe ceremony—divesting me of my boot and holding it long in his hand, looking at it with eyes at once critical and loving, as if recalling the glow with which he had created it, and rebuking the way in which one had disorganized this masterpiece. Then, placing my foot on a piece of paper, he would two or three times tickle the outer edges with a pencil and pass his nervous fingers over my toes, feeling himself into the heart of my requirement.

I cannot forget that day on which I had occasion to say to him: "Mr. Gessler, that last pair of town walking boots creaked, you know."

He looked at me for a time without replying, as if expecting me to withdraw or qualify the statement, then said:

"Id shouldn'd 'ave greaked."

"It did, I'm afraid."

"You goddem wed before dey found demselves?"

"I don't think so."

At that he lowered his eyes, as if hunting for memory of those boots, and I felt sorry I had mentioned this grave thing.

"Zend dem back!" he said. "I will look at dem."

A feeling of compassion for my creaking boots surged up in me, so well could I imagine the sorrowful long curiosity of regard which he would bend on them.

"Zome boods," he said slowly, "are bad from birdt. If I can do noding wid dem, I dake dem off your bill."

Once (once only) I went absent-mindedly into his shop in a pair of boots bought in an emergency at some large firm's. He took my order without showing me any leather, and I could feel his eyes penetrating the inferior integument of my foot.

At last he said, "Dose are nod my boods."

The tone was not one of anger, nor of sorrow, not even of contempt, but there was in it something quiet that froze the blood. He put his hand down and pressed a finger on the place where the left boot, endeavoring to be fashionable, was not quite comfortable.

"Id 'urds you dere," he said. "Dose big virms 'ave no self-respect. Drash!" And then, as if something had given way within him, he spoke long and bitterly. It was the only time I ever heard him discuss the conditions and hardships of his trade.

"Dey ged id all," he said, "dey ged id by adverdisement, nod by work. Dey dake id away from us, who lofe our boods. Id gomes to this—bresently I haf no work. Every year id gets less—you will see." And looking at his lined face I saw things I had never noticed before, bitter things and bitter struggle—and what a lot of gray hairs there seemed suddenly in his red beard!

As best I could, I explained the circumstances of the purchase of those ill-omened boots. But his face and voice made so deep an impression that during the next few minutes I ordered many pairs. Nemesis fell! They lasted more terribly than ever. And I was not able conscientiously to go to him for nearly two years.

When at last I went I was surprised to find that outside one of the two little windows of his shop another name was painted, also that of a bootmaker—making, of course, for the Royal Family. The old familiar boots, no longer in dignified isolation, were huddled in the single window. Inside, the now contracted well of the one little shop was more scented and darker than ever. And it was longer than usual, too, before a face peered down, and the tip-tap of the bast slippers began. At last he stood before me, and, gazing through those rusty iron spectacles, said:

"Mr. ———, isn't it?"

"Ah! Mr. Gessler," I stammered, "but your boots are really *too* good, you know! See, these are quite decent still!" And I stretched out to him my foot. He looked at it.

"Yes," he said, "beople do nod wand good boods, id seems."

To get away from his reproachful eyes and voice I hastily remarked: "What have you done to your shop?"

He answered quietly, "Id was too exbensif. Do you wand some boods?"

I ordered three pairs, though I had only wanted two, and quickly left. I had, I know not quite what feeling of being part, in his mind, of a conspiracy against him; or not perhaps so much against him as against his idea of boot. One does not, I suppose, care to feel like that; for it was again many months before my next visit to his shop, paid I remember, with the feeling: *Oh! well, I can't leave the old boy—so here goes! Perhaps it'll be his elder brother!*

For his elder brother, I knew, had not character enough to reproach me, even silently.

And, to my relief, in the shop there did appear to be his elder brother, handling a piece of leather.

"Well, Mr. Gessler," I said, "how are you?"

He came close and peered at me.

"I am breddy well," he said slowly, "but my elder brudder is dead."

And I saw that it was indeed himself—but how aged and wan! And never before had I heard him mention his brother.

Much shocked, I murmured, "Oh—I am sorry."

"Yes," he answered, "he was a good man, he made a good bood; but he is dead." And he touched the top of his head, where the hair had suddenly gone as thin as it had been on that of his poor brother, to indicate, I suppose, the cause of his death. "He could nod ged over losing the oder shop. Do you wand any boods?" And he held up the leather in his hand. "Id's a beaudiful biece."

I ordered several pairs. It was very long before they came—but they were better than ever. One simply could not wear them out. And soon after that I went abroad.

It was over a year before I was again in London. And the first shop I went to was my old friend's. I had left a man of sixty, I came back to one of seventy-five, pinched and worn and tremulous, who genuinely, this time, did not at first know me.

"Oh! Mr. Gessler," I said, sick at heart, "how splendid your boots are! See, I've been wearing this pair nearly all the time I've been abroad; and they're not half worn out, are they?"

He looked long at my boots—a pair of Russia leather, and his face seemed to regain steadiness. Putting his hand on my instep, he said, "Do dey vid you here? I 'ad drouble wid dat bair, I remember." I assured him that they fit beautifully.

"Do you wand any boods?" he said. "I can make dem quickly; id is a slack dime."

I answered, "Please, please! I want boots all around—every kind!"

"I will make a vresh model. Your food must be bigger." And with utter slowness, he traced round my foot, and felt my toes, only once looking up to say, "Did I tell you my brudder was dead?"

To watch him was painful, so feeble had he grown. I was glad to get away.

I had given those boots up, when one evening they came. Opening the parcel, I set the four pairs out in a row. Then one by one I tried them on. There was no doubt about it: in shape and fit, in finish and quality of leather, they were the best he had ever made me. And in the mouth of one of the town walking boots I found his bill. The amount was the same as usual, but it gave me quite a shock. He had never before sent it in till quarter day. I flew downstairs and wrote a cheque, and posted it at once with my own hand.

A week later, passing the little street, I thought I would go in and tell him how splendidly the new boots fitted. But when I came to where his shop had been, his name was gone. Still there, in the window, were the slim pumps, the patent leathers with cloth tops, the sooty riding boots.

I went in, very much disturbed. In the two little shops—again made into one—was a young man with an English face.

"Mr. Gessler in?" I said.

He gave me a strange, ingratiating look.

"No, sir," he said, "no. But we can attend to anything with pleasure. We've taken the shop over. You've seen our name, no doubt, next door. We make for some very good people."

"Yes, yes," I said, "but Mr. Gessler?"

"Oh!" he answered. "Dead."

"Dead! But I only received these boots from him last Wednesday week."

"Ah!" he said, "a shockin' go. Poor old man starved 'imself."

"What!"

"Slow starvation, the doctor called it! You see he went to work in such a way! Would keep the shop on; wouldn't have a soul touch his boots except himself. When he got an order, it took him such a time. People won't wait. He lost everybody. And there he'd sit, goin' on and on—I will say that for him—not a man in London made a better boot! But look at the competition! He never advertised! Would 'ave the best leather, too, and do it all 'imself. Well, there it is. What could you expect with his ideas?"

"But starvation—"

"That may be a bit flowery, as the sayin' is, but I know myself he was sittin' over his boots day and night, to the very last. You see I used to watch him. Never gave 'imself time to eat; never had a penny in the house. All went in rent and leather. How he lived so long I don't know. He regular let his fire go out. He was a character. But he made good boots."

"Yes," I said, "he made good boots."

And I turned and went out quickly, for I did not want him to know that I could hardly see.

JOHN GALSWORTHY (1867–1933), *English novelist, playwright, and poet, was awarded the Nobel Prize in Literature in 1932. He is best known for his* Forsyte Saga.

A Good Name
or Great Riches

Frank Hampton

The suave young man was ready to leave the country. The bank's depositors would just have to take their lumps. Then into the bank walked his father.

"Tell me all about it, Jim," was all he said.

No other story I have ever read so clearly mirrors the difference between Americans as they once were (standards of integrity) and Americans today, most of whom apparently believe that there is no longer such a thing as right or wrong. If your attorney can get you off the hook, that's all that counts. This story reminds us that it wasn't always that way.

———————

As I turned away from the grave that afternoon in early spring, I heard someone say, "When I die, I wish you'd ask that minister to officiate at my funeral."

I turned to see who had made so singular a request, and met

the gaze of the old gentleman whose fine face and shabby clothes had attracted my attention before the funeral when I met a group of businessmen who had come up to Sioux Falls from a little town over the line in an adjoining state. These men from a neighboring state had come up to Sioux Falls to pay their last tribute of respect to the memory of an old gentleman who had been well known for many years in financial circles.

I soon forgot the incident at the grave. Late that autumn a message came requesting me to come down to the little town in Iowa to conduct the funeral of the old gentleman who had expressed the wish that I might render such a service.

I took the train Saturday afternoon and arrived in the little town a full hour before time for the funeral. They drove me to the little cottage on the hill where the deceased had lived for many years. After I had spoken a few words of comfort to his aged wife, a big man, in whose dark hair streaks of gray were beginning to show, asked me to step into the room where the dead man lay.

We stood silent beside the dead for a full minute; then the big man broke down. His body shook with sobs such as a strong man surrenders to when moved by a mighty emotion. Regaining his composure, he said: "He's my father, sir. Look at those hands." He lifted the hard, rough, callused right hand. "I caused it all," he continued. "My father was one of the wealthiest men in this part of the state. He owned four fine farms. He moved to town, but drove to the country every day to oversee the work on the farms.

"I was president and cashier of the one bank in town. I married and built me a nice home. I was making money and was considered one of the progressive men of the community. At first I

confided to my father my business methods and paying transactions. Later he began to expostulate with me about certain risks I was taking with what he insisted on calling 'other folks' money.'

"I didn't like his criticism; so I stopped telling him about the big deals. I think he knew I was withholding important matters from him. He had a hurt look that troubled me. I justified my changed attitude toward him by saying to myself, *There's big money in it. Father's too old to understand; when I'm a rich man, he'll see that I was right.*"

There was another pause. The big man bowed his head on the coffin and sobbed. Recovering himself, he resumed his story, realizing that in a few minutes the friends would come in and interrupt us, and he was anxious to finish his narrative.

Wiping his eyes with a handkerchief, he resumed: "Well, sir, a day came when the market went against me, wiping out everything I had and, worst of all, leaving the bank fifty thousand dollars short. Money was close. I wired Minneapolis for money. Nothing doing there. I called Sioux City on long distance, and received a curt refusal.

"I was desperate. My temple of fortune had been built on sand, and when the financial storm struck it, everything collapsed, burying me beneath the ruins. Just before closing time, Father came in. He knew something was wrong. When the hands of the clock pointed to a minute of three, I closed the door, bolted it, and drew down the shades. Father took my arm, and silently we walked into the rear room.

" 'Tell me all about it, Jim,' was all he said.

"I told him all. 'Father, I've been a fool,' I said in conclusion.

" 'What do you plan to do, Jim?' Father inquired when I had finished.

"'I'm going to leave. Monday morning will see me well on my way to the great Northwest,' I said.

"'That would be criminal, Jim; you mustn't run away from failure. You must stay here until we can settle up the affairs of the bank. Every depositor must have his money, dollar for dollar.'

"'But, Father,' I protested, 'the bank has failed. I've lost my money and your money; the depositors will have to stand their share.'

"'They trusted you, Jim, because the Crosby name has always been a guarantee for integrity. A good name, Jim, can't be sacrificed. I'll take the afternoon train for Sioux Falls; if I fail there, I'll take the midnight train for Minneapolis. *Somewhere* I'll find the money.'

"'Father,' I exclaimed, as I saw him taking a bunch of blank farm mortgages from the desk, 'what do you plan to do?'

"'Why, the only thing I can do, Jim: mortgage my farms.'

"I could not induce him to change his plan. He mortgaged everything he had. Every depositor was paid in full. I left soon after for the far Northwest. I never wanted to see this town again. I'm here now because—because I *had* to see his face again. The financial Depression that followed rendered it impossible for Father to redeem those mortgages. He lost *everything*. I never dreamed of the depths of poverty to which he was reduced. For five years he's been janitor down at the bank! Yet no man in this county is more respected than my father. And here I thought a man couldn't be anything without money. A good name is—sir, what does the Bible say?"

"'A good name is rather to be chosen than great riches,'" I replied.

"Yes, that's it; every business house in town will close for

Father's funeral. Did you notice the chairs in the yard? There's not a room in town that'd hold the crowd that will be here, so the funeral will be in the open air."

That crowd was already gathering in the yard. Jim Crosby gave me his hand, saying, "I just wanted to tell you, sir, so that you can tell young men about the worth of a good name."

Nothing is known about FRANK HAMPTON.

THE CIRCLE
IN THE FIRE

Leonard C. Lee

"Stay right here until I come back!" That was the command. But then his clothes began to burn, and his hair caught fire. What should he do?

It was a beautiful autumn day in North Dakota. The prairie grass was so rank and tall that even with my nearly five years of sturdy growth I could barely see over it. The prairie stretched for miles in every direction, dotted here and there with a fresh-plowed field, a lonely farmhouse, or a struggling grove of stunted trees. On one side was the broken country along the James River that had never been touched by a plow.

My father was plowing about a mile from home with my grandfather's team of five big black horses. I often went to meet him near quitting time, and he would put me on one of the horses to ride. "I didn't fall off," I told my mother proudly, "I just hung on to the feathers."

One day I started a bit early and was nearly to the field, wading through the tall prairie grass, when I heard the horses coming. Their hoofbeats were like thunder. Then I saw them. They were coming right at me, running like mad. I could see Daddy standing up on the plow swinging a long whip. Daddy was whipping the horses. I was so frightened I couldn't move. The lead horses saw me and shied to one side, and Daddy caught a glimpse of yellow curls in the tall grass as he careened past. I caught just a flash of his face as he turned to see what the horses shied at. I had never seen my daddy look like that before.

I watched, fascinated, as he swung the team in a wide arc. He tripped the plow into the ground and plowed three double furrows around me. Then he stopped the plow and set fire to the grass inside the plowed furrows in a dozen places. He picked me up and held me while he burned off all the grass in the circle. Then he drew a small circle right in the middle of the burned area and put me in it.

"Stay right here until I come back." he said. There was a sharpness in his voice that I had never heard before. His face was white and drawn and desperate. I knew that he meant exactly what he said and that I had better obey.

It had taken only seconds to accomplish his mission. His tall, thin body worked with the precision of a machine. There was a terrible urgency about him that I could not understand. He jumped on the plow, swung the whip, and I was left alone.

I didn't know, and he couldn't take time to tell me, that the prairie was on fire and that the flames were racing right for our

home. Daddy was hurrying to put black plowed earth between the fire and his loved ones.

With a shock of horror that almost knocked him off the plow, he saw me, his oldest son, his pride and joy, standing alone on the burning prairie. Daddy couldn't take me with him, and other lives were in more peril than I was. His only hope was my obedience.

I stayed in my circle a bit unwillingly. My father was a Norwegian and a strict disciplinarian. We children had been taught to obey. I was unconscious of danger and curious that so many small animals were coming out of the grass into my blackened circle. There were gophers and mice and snakes and birds. A coyote came in, took a good look at me, and went on. A jack rabbit almost as large as I was tried to share my small circle. His hair was badly singed, and he seemed to want me to help him.

I soon began to smell smoke, and the air got hot and hard to breathe. Then I saw the fire coming. The flames made a sound like that of a freight train. I wanted to run, but Daddy had said, "Stay right here until I come back." I tried to claw into the ground, but the sod was thick, and tough. Tongues of flame like giant arms kept reaching out for me.

My clothes started to burn, and my hair burned. I rolled on the ground and screamed and clawed at the earth. Then I felt the earth shaking with the thud of pounding hoofs, and I knew that Daddy was coming. The next thing I remember, I was in my father's arms.

Daddy had saved our home with the help of neighbors who came from miles around with barrels of water and brooms and blankets and teams and plows. Then he swung his tired team around and lashed them into foaming furies in a race to reach me ahead of the fire. Fearing he was too late, but clinging to a desperate hope, he drove his terrified horses through a wall of flame into my circle and found me right in the middle of the circle where he had left me.

Many a night after that when I would awake screaming and clawing as from a terrible dream, I would find myself in my father's arms. His love and tenderness would still my terror. He would take me with him into his own bed, and I would fall asleep secure with him close by my side.

As I grew older I learned that God is a loving Father. My own experience helped me to understand God's love and protection. My father saw the destruction coming and made a place of safety for me. But I was safe only if I obeyed. I would have perished in the flames if I had not stayed in my circle. My father did all he could, but I had to do my part by obeying the one who knew the only way in which I could be safe.

LEONARD C. LEE *wrote for popular American magazines such as* The Saturday Evening Post *during the first third of the twentieth century. Today, little is known about him.*

PART II

HOPE

*And we rejoice in the hope of the glory of God. Not only so,
but we also rejoice in our sufferings, because we know
that suffering produces perseverance; perseverance, character;
and character, hope. And hope does not disappoint us,
because God has poured out his love into our hearts
by the Holy Spirit, whom he has given us.*

ROMANS 5:2-5

THE MISSING WORD

G. E. *Wallace*

Dr. Jordan Ashley, a physician of note, served on this board and on that one. He was a very busy man and would say to each caller "by his manner if not by his words, 'I can give you only a little time.'"

All this Alice Bennet suddenly realized, and was almost panic-stricken: for he represented her only hope of getting that coveted scholarship.

It was strange what small things could upset your world. Alice Bennet was thinking of that as she sat trying to put the parts of her broken world together. It was queer what sort of small things—a telephone call, a telegraph messenger, an item in the newspaper.

It had been that last in her case—just an inch or two of financial news, bad news, and her world had collapsed. She couldn't go back to the university in the fall—unless—

Alice sat at her desk, frowning. There were some things you couldn't change—for instance, the fact that her father's fortune was lost. But a thoroughbred could stand adversity, and fight it.

Alice began to consider what things were left that were still in her favor. There was her physical well-being. That counted greatly. She was strong. She could work. And then there was the fact that she had had two years in college. Neither that nor the record she had made there could be taken from her. Out of a class of three thousand she had stood among the upper ten. And then there were her friends, and the friends of her family.

Alice's eyes narrowed. Friends. She sat and thought over the friends she had and those her father had. She began to write down names on a piece of paper. There was Williams, a storekeeper. He could give her work. But she didn't want the kind of work he could offer. Clerking at eighteen dollars a week did not appeal to her. She was going to gain wealth!

The list of names on the paper grew longer. And suddenly Alice Bennet started. There before her was the solution to her problem. She felt elated. Even if the family fortune had crumbled, she could start—and climb, and climb! She was no weakling!

The last name she had written on the paper was "Dr. Jordan Ashley."

————

Dr. Jordan Ashley was an elderly man, a busy man. He was a physician of note. He served on this board and that board. And besides, he had his charity patients to care for, although few knew of those patients. So Dr. Jordon Ashley said, by his manner if not by his words, "I can give you only a little time."

Alice sensed his desire to make the interview short. For a moment she was panic-stricken. In her own room, when she was planning what she would say, she had had control of the interview from the start. Now she seemed to have lost that control.

"I know your father—well," Dr. Ashley said.

And he seemed to be saying, "Please hurry!"

"So I came to you," Alice added inanely. Then she fought for her self-possession, and gained it. He wanted a short interview, a businesslike interview. Very well, she would get right to the point.

"You see," she explained, "Father has suffered a financial loss, and I'm afraid I can't go back to the university—unless—"

"Yes?" Dr. Jordon Ashley was noncommittal. He was on the board of trustees. Besides, he was a member of the Alumni Club.

"Unless," Alice Bennet said, "I am given a scholarship that will pay all my expenses.

Dr. Jordon Ashley kept still.

"Which you can award," Alice Bennet added.

Dr. Jordon Ashley did not deny or affirm the fact.

"And so I came to you. And I want that scholarship because I deserve it—not because Father is an old friend of yours."

Dr. Jordon Ashley seemed pleased. And if Alice had known how many wanted scholarships given to them because of their need alone, and how many applicants thought they deserved this consideration simply because they were needy, she might have known how really pleased he was.

"Why do you think you deserve a scholarship?" Dr. Jordon Ashley asked.

And Alice proceeded to give him facts and figures. There were three thousand in her class; she had ranked tenth. "And I know," she said, "that none of the nine who rank above me want the scholarship, or have taken the studies that qualify them to apply for it."

The scholarship was unique in that it was given to a junior who had finished the premedical course, and it was good for five years. It paid the student's way through his collegiate course, and through the medical school of the university.

"I," Alice Bennet explained, "have taken the premedical course."

"Why did you?"

Alice was startled.

"Why?"

She was honest. She had taken it because she was interested in science, and not in literature or the classics. And she said so.

"You had not considered medicine seriously as a profession before your father's financial loss?"

"No."

Dr. Jordon Ashley sat there and studied the girl before him.

"Well," he finally said, "that does not disqualify you." He seemed to be trying to puzzle something out.

"I hoped it would not."

"Why are you interested in medicine now?"

And she knew the answer. A specialist in medicine could make money! She would. "It's a well-paid profession," she answered.

"Yes," Dr. Jordon Ashley sighed. "It *is* a well-paid profession."

"And I have the ability."

Dr. Jordon Ashley did not say she could have the scholarship that was his to bestow. Neither did he say she could not have it. He lifted the receiver of the phone, put through a long-distance call, and finally scribbled a name on a piece of paper.

"There's been a flood in that district," he said. "Doctor Wendell [the name on the paper] is in charge. He's a keen man, and an eminent physician."

She had heard of him.

"If you'll go down there—and prove what you can do—"

She left the office smiling happily.

There was mud, slimy mud, everywhere. On the streets the men used fire hoses to wash it off. In the houses they used workers.

Alice worked. She had thought she was strong—and she *was* strong—but she was weary, too, unutterably weary. There was mud, and slime, and filth!

Doctor Wendell was keen and capable. Doctor Wendell was impersonal. He saw the filth, and the slime, and the tasks that had to be done.

If, Alice Bennet thought, *I had no education, I could serve just as well.* For her task was to scrub, and scrub, and see that disinfectant reached the places where disinfectant had to go.

Pictures of nurses in clean white uniforms were a mockery. Tales of nurses soothing children came to her mind and made her laugh—at her ignorance. Why, if the children of the district were one half as clean as the cherubs that were depicted in stories, or on the posters, they would not need the services of a nurse.

You did not use what knowledge you had; you scrubbed! You did not use initiative—you carried out orders.

The hours passed, long hours. And days became weeks.

I'll quit! Alice Bennet thought. What was the sense of staying? Dr. Jordon Ashley would be expecting to hear of the wonderful work she had done, of how her laboratory technique had helped. He would not care to hear about her scrubbing, and washing, and scrubbing.

"You are to report to 110 River Street. Go from there to 29 Front Street, and clean up those places," Doctor Wendell said.

"Yes, sir."

But she would not go! She would pack up and return home!

"After you have finished, call me. There are some other houses to clean."

He did not seem to know that it was a test; that she had been sent to prove that she was worthy of the scholarship which would start her on the road to wealth!

"That's all."

She turned. She had been tempted to say, "Can't I work in the supply depot—or help in that laboratory you've set up—or assist in the emergency hospital?" But Doctor Wendell was impersonal.

She walked, rebellion in her heart, down the street, past the squads of workers busy at the task of getting a city back on its feet. They did not bother to look up. They recognized her as a fellow worker, but they did not care.

She would go back home—away from the mud, and the squalor, and the unfortunates who were anything but grateful.

There had been a man who had threatened her because she had insisted on enforcing some rules that called for the destruction of certain water-soaked possessions. And then there had been a woman— She stopped, for what that woman in yonder doorway was doing was not what should be done with a child who had suffered exposure.

The woman was ignorant, pathetically ignorant.

Alice walked on down the street. The woman was ignorant, as were so many others—hopeless, befuddled.

She worked. And always there was the mud, and the stench, and the slime.

Doctor Wendell came down in his car to take her from Front Street to Avenue B. And Avenue B was worse.

"I sort of thought..." Doctor Wendell said—but he did not finish.

He did not suggest in the days that followed that she ought to serve in any spectacular way. He just saw that she was moved, first here, then there, wherever there was mud.

Once he did say that she seemed cheerful.

She stood before him, bedraggled, dirty, her hands red and raw. "I am," she said.

Dr. Jordon Ashley was a busy man. He had his practice, and he served on this board and that. But Dr. Jordon Ashley did not hurry Alice Bennet as she told him of her work in the flooded area.

"And you still would like the scholarship and would like to study medicine!" Doctor Ashley asked.

"Yes."

"Why?"

Before—well, before, she had been truthful. She had said, frankly, that a specialist could make money. She would be truthful again, although maybe Doctor Ashley would think her queer.

"I would like to study," she said, "to fit myself for service."

"'Open sesame!'" Doctor Jordon Ashley said, with a broad smile.

"Pardon? I didn't quite get that," Alice Bennet said.

"It's the word I wanted to hear," Doctor Ashley said, "the word that was lacking the last time—*service*."

And once again, from Dr. Jordon Ashley's office, Alice Bennet walked out smiling.

G. E. WALLACE's *niche was unique: stories dealing with that intangible line between success and failure, in terms of both career and lifestyle. Little is known about him (or her) as a person or writer except that most of his (or her) stories were first published during the first third of the twentieth century.*

THE RED GERANIUM

Viola M. Payne

Mother sacrificed her loveliest flower for a sorrowing neighbor—
for more, in fact, than that neighbor's grief alone.

When I thought of the Miles family before that March morning,
it was with vague superiority. They were new to our southwestern
community, having recently rented a river farm consisting of sandy,
scrub-oak thickets—an unhappy contrast to the more fertile land
around my home. And if my girlish life at seventeen sometimes
seemed bleak, at least I was spared the elemental struggles of such
families.

My mother was bending over a geranium growing under our
living room window. Its large flower had blossomed in a vivid
color—rosy-scarlet, with an iridescent glow. Mother raised beautiful houseplants, but this was the most striking she had ever grown.

"Why can't something exciting happen?" I asked. "Even a
funeral would be better than having *nowhere* to go."

Mother's startled gaze followed me out the door, where peach blossoms spilled hesitant fragrance. Suddenly a car stopped in front of our house. The driver spoke to Mother and hurriedly left.

"Bad news from the Miles family," she explained sadly. "Their week-old baby girl died last night."

I shrugged. "They're probably better off. They still have seven children left."

Mother evaded my remark. "We should go over there, but we won't have the car today. Would you walk?"

"Me? Why?"

"Because I ask you to. I would like you to take a flower."

"A flower? But we have nothing to give but peach blossoms, and those seem kind of out of place for a funeral."

Then I realized where mother's gaze was traveling. She picked up scissors and started toward the red geranium.

"No!" I protested. "You can't send *it*. It's the loveliest flower anywhere around. You've cared for the thing all winter. You'll never have such a flower again."

Mother quickly clipped the stem beneath the bloom. While I watched in stunned silence, she surrounded it with asparagus fern and decorated the spray with a white bow.

"I suppose I might as well take it," I sighed, "but it seems such a waste."

With the flower in a shoebox I walked north and cut cross-country. Beyond the river the Miles house crouched against a sand dune. Inside the kitchen neighbors greeted me quietly. A daughter, Esther, smiled. Her clothing, although old, was neat. The house, I noticed, was also spotlessly clean.

"I have a flower here," I handed her the box.

She lifted the lid quickly, and was so moved that she could scarcely answer. "It's so nice of you to bring it. You see, this is the only flower we have."

I was shocked. Not that we were used to lavish funeral displays, but there had always been wreaths.

"Let's show Mother."

Hesitantly I followed her to where a pale, worn woman lay in bed. A tear glistened on one of her cheeks, but she tried to smile at me.

"Look, Mother—she brought a flower for the baby."

When Mrs. Miles opened the box, some of the glow from the flower seemed to light her face. She touched the bloom gently, as if it were a sacred thing. "How lovely. I was hoping that my baby would have at least one flower."

I felt tears spring into my eyes. This was a new insight into mother love. What a strange thing—it could be divided without diminishing!

"Would you like to see the baby?" Esther asked.

We entered a room where there was a sheet-covered bench. Diffused light touched the simple little casket resting upon it. The baby had the look of a translucent china doll. She was fine of feature, with a wide brow. She might have done great things...she might have...

I moved away. Inside the kitchen I tried to make conversation with the women preparing food. But I could no longer be casual about the Miles baby. She had become a personality to me, not just some unknown creature gone to an ageless sleep. The mystery of life and death seemed shrouded in that small, fragile frame.

At midafternoon our little group stood quietly in the community cemetery. Heavy veils of cloud darkened the sun. The wind was rising; it fluttered the pages of the Bible in the minister's hands and whistled across the tiny grave before us.

Had I stayed away from the Miles family, I reflected, it might have been easy to remain indifferent to their troubles. But here I was beside them, with tears to match their own.

I glanced toward the wooden cross marking the grave. The red geranium lay at its feet, with petals beginning to shrivel and blacken. How drab our living room must look without the bright bloom! But suddenly I understood, along with my mother, that one flower was a small price to pay for teaching her daughter compassion.

Nothing is known about VIOLA M. PAYNE *except that she wrote for inspirational magazines in the early to mid–twentieth century.*

HILDA'S TROUSSEAU

Florence Crannell Means

There were just the two of them, mother and daughter—and now Stan. They were so poor, and Stan's family so well-to-do. Fortunately, Hilda had five years in which to put together her wedding trousseau. The mother could handle poverty, even the gradual loss of her eyesight. What she could not handle without heartbreak was to have no part in the trousseau.

But finally came the day when the trousseau could be hidden no longer.

All through breakfast, spring sunshine had poured gayly through the wavy window glass and dappled the worn linoleum and the patched tablecloth. But Hilda's words quenched its pale radiance and chilled its warmth; the kitchen went dull and gray before Mrs. Trask's eyes.

"Mother, darling," Hilda asked hesitantly, "don't you think all the—all the shopping we had planned would be dreadful hard for you? I—I've been wondering whether it wouldn't be better for me to take Marian instead; she'll be glad to go, she says."

A mere friend to share that splendid orgy, instead of her own mother! "Why, the idea!" Mrs. Trask protested. "You act as if I were an invalid or something!" She straightened her small, thin body capably. "I wouldn't miss it for anything. Not for anything, Hilda!"

Hilda flushed unhappily. "But Mother, I thought—I'd like to see—just how sensibly and well I could choose things; I want to—I want to choose my trousseau—all by myself. Seems as if I've never had the handling of a bit of money, not a bit. How am I going to know how to handle—Stan's?"

That was true. The meager wages she earned at the small town library and the money her mother wrested from the world with her washtub and iron, all had gone scrupulously into a common treasury, a treasury that Mrs. Trask had apportioned with the minutest care, to their debts, to their common needs, to the trousseau fund.

She had never dreamed, though, that Hilda could snatch away her share in the harvest of their years of self-denial, although everyone had warned her that children were like that. "You'll find out some day!" they had prophesied with gloomy assurance. "If a mother wants to work her fingers to the bone for her children, she has herself to thank."

Scornfully Mrs. Trask had maintained that Hilda was different. But perhaps she had been mistaken. Perhaps she was wrong, and everyone else was right.

"You won't care, Mother?"

Mrs. Trask shook her head, looking fixedly down into her plate and picking at her milk toast with a fork that shook blurrily before her eyes. Hilda kissed her silently, and went away to her day's work. Still she sat there, hands limp in her lap, thin shoulders drooped. One could not measure the blow the words had dealt, unless one knew what the buying of that trousseau had meant to them both.

To Mrs. Trask, who did fine laundry for the town's rich folk, it had been at once a wonderful and a terrifying thing that her Hilda should be asked in marriage by Stanley Armstrong, the prosperous attorney's son. In the small town high school where they met, Hilda's gentle manners and tall dark loveliness moved on a sort of social equality with the more favored of fortune, and even the simplicity of her wardrobe was not a serious inconvenience. Her home was shabby enough, but Mrs. Trask had contrived with an ingenuity that was fiercely determined, had sacrificed with an intensity of purpose that was passionate, to make the living room a place of quaint charm for Hilda's friends, especially for Hilda's eager-eyed young Stan. Hilda should not be ashamed! Hilda should never have to be embarrassed or apologetic!

The wedding had been a problem, for the little house would never do for the reception of Stan's family in all its important ramifications, and Stan's friends. Only since Hilda had finished high school had they paid off the heavy mortgage it carried.

They had not been able to put any money into repairs, for illness and death had saddled them with monstrous old debts that chafed their scrupulous spirits.

But while the cottage had grown dilapidated, the yard had grown lovely. While the shingles had split and curled and the paint had flaked and the porch had sagged, the trees had towered tall and the lilac and spirea had spread wide arms, the woodbine and the roses had hung mantles of green and bloom. The yard solved the problem; the wedding bower was to be set in its shaded retreats. As long ago as last summer Hilda had begun to build for it with skillful care. The chrysanthemums that she had transplanted there would be blossoming into a swaying semicircle of green and gold and white when the wedding day came; goldenrod would raise its spires of dusky gold behind them; dahlias would weave an array of flaming color. No one could wish anything lovelier than the garden wedding would be, on a blue and gold September day.

Nor need they fear any patronizing inspection of Hilda's dower chest. There had been time to fill it to the brim during the five years of waiting while Stan went on through the university, to come out to establish himself in business, and while Hilda worked in the public library. Snowy things, frosted with delicate monograms and tatting; sturdy utilitarian linens.

Now it was May, and only the trousseau remained to be planned. "Six of everything," Mrs. Trask had insisted, "and the wedding gown; and a silk one, and a serge; and a little afternoon dress; and a half-dozen good ginghams. Two hats—two! And three pairs of shoes besides the wedding slippers."

They had decided on the sum that would be adequate, with the kind of shopping and contriving that the thrifty poor have learned. It was a larger sum than they would have needed if everything could have been made at home. But Mrs. Trask could not sew—her eyesight was fast growing too dim for even her fine laundry work—and she had not taught Hilda. Many of the garments must be purchased ready-made, though some Hilda herself would make at the evening sewing classes of the Opportunity School. Penny by penny, dime by dime, dollar by dollar, they had plodded toward the goal without a shadow of turning, until they had attained it.

Meanwhile they had gone clothed in shreds and patches. A whole outer layer, to be sure, was essential for Hilda, working in the public eye; but Mrs. Trask's one "decent" dress was worn threadbare at every seam and shiny in between, and there was a patch at each elbow. It was fortunate that she knew a bakery where sugar sacks still sold for five cents each. Sugar-sack lingerie is sturdy stuff; it will take unto itself patch beside patch and patch upon patch before it gives up the struggle in despair, completely surrenders its identity as a garment and becomes a mop rag.

It had all been worthwhile, with the promise of that delirium of buying to shine at the end of the avenue of meager years. She and Hilda had planned to take this garnered wealth of theirs and go on a grand expedition of shopping—such as had never been known. All these years they had planned for it; and now—

Hilda's words re-echoed in her ears: "I want to choose my trousseau—all by myself!" She had thought her daughter and herself marvelously one. She had thought even marriage could not mar the relationship—much. And Stanley was enough like the fairytale prince to please any reasonable mother. But now—

Resolutely Mrs. Trask stiffened her lips with a smile. It was only youth! And youth, they say, is always selfish. She rose listlessly and cleared away the breakfast things. This had taken the tuck out of her more than yesterday's ten hours of ironing.

The summer days wore on, crowded full for them both. More work fell on Mrs. Trask's shoulders, of necessity, for Hilda's hours at home were brim-full of billowing white things, orchid things, beige, peach—a flower garden done in fabrics. All day at the library, three evenings a week at the sewing class, betweenwhiles stitch-stitch-stitching, fine seams and delicate embroideries. She sewed while her mother ironed, while her mother washed dishes; but she swept a towel around her handiwork when any one came too near. It was to burst upon the admiring eyes as a grand exhibit, a perfect whole, she said. She said it eagerly, coaxingly, searching her mother's face with eyes that pleaded for pardon. After all, she could have no idea what it was to be shut out so from this great event of a daughter's life; she could not mean to hurt so deeply.

Stan was suffering too. Hilda granted his big impatience only an evening a week and the little time it took to drive her to the library in the morning and home at night in his purring roadster.

"Such a little while!" she soothed him, as she shook her needle-pricked fingers in mock wrath. "And, Stan, please don't scold about the sewing. I'm just all weepy inside now, and cross! I'm so tired of needles and thread."

August! Still and sweet and simmering in amber sunshine. Hilda was working feverishly now; every evening she brought home a parcel or two and tucked them into a big box beneath her bed. Her mother looked at the box curiously when she swept Hilda's room, but she neither touched the parcels nor asked about them. She didn't ask about anything. Hilda laughed at her a little uncertainly one day.

"You've planned everything about the wedding, even which chrysanthemum I'm to stand in front of, but you seem to have forgotten that the bride's mother will be among those present. What do you plan on wearing, little Mother?"

"It looks as if I'll wear my best apron and stand behind the lilac bush till it's time to serve the ice cream and patties and things." Mrs. Trask's laugh was mirthless.

Hilda kissed her lightly. "We'll manage a little dress somehow. There'll be sales this month," she promised. *Just like a mother putting off an importunate child,* Mrs. Trask thought resentfully. *No, no. She mustn't feel so about Hilda; Hilda, who had never been anything but tender. She was tired out now and unsteadied by the heavy draft of those joyous, overfull days.*

September! Golden September, with mountains blue and silver through the crystal miles of air.

"Mother," Hilda announced after the dishpan had been hung away one fragrant evening, "I have the pleasure of inviting you to inspect my trousseau at precisely this o'clock. The underthings are here," she explained, as she threw wide her bedroom door, "but the dresses and the other things are in the living room, where Stan can see them too, when he comes pretty soon."

The plain little room had blossomed into exotic color. Orchid, sea-green, peach, beige, powder-blue, white, they foamed across the bed. Mrs. Trask's heart contracted with joy and pain. It was good to wear sugar sacks forever and a day that her child might go to her new home with so brave a store of finery.

"They're—beautiful!" Vainly she sought words for them as her hard fingertips caressed their delicacy. "You've done wonderfully, daughter. But"—her voice held something of anxiety—"some of them look so—skimpy. Are you sure they're large enough?"

"Plenty large enough. You can look at them more after a while, Mother. There's Stan closing the gate now, and I'm so anxious to know how you'll like the dresses in the other room."

When Stan came in, she turned them both to face the double doorway that led into the dining room. She had swept the portières aside and hung the garments from the wooden pole.

A cloak, deep-piled and lustrous. "Isn't it nice?" she demanded. "I got it way back in March, in Lane's big spring sale, and they kept it in the 'will call' for me until you gave me the money." A slim frock of heavy silk crepe, a flaming-colored wisp of an afternoon gown; smart ginghams, yellow, and blue, and apricot. The wedding gown.

"I wanted it plain, Mother," Hilda explained eagerly, as her mother fingered its clinging ivory fabric. "You do like it?"

"It's lovely," her mother agreed, "with that long embroidered panel. No wonder your eyes are tired, Hilda."

A little hat, at once *chic* and serviceable; white satin slippers, slender and long like Hilda; smart tan pumps; plain black ones with an ankle strap.

"But where are the other things? That isn't all?"

"No, that isn't all." Hilda wheeled her mother around toward the couch, spread with more finery.

Another cloak, luxuriously fur-collared. ("I found I could get two for the price of one, at the sale!") A slip of a frock, soft gray, with cobweb lace at the neck. Trim ginghams, gray, and blue, and tan. A hat that lifted a crest of lace and dignity. Trim black slippers.

Mrs. Trask questioned them with blank eyes. Lifted the slippers.

"They're—they're much too small!" she faltered. "All—these—are away too small, Hilda."

"No, I don't think they are," Hilda dissented, "but we'll try them on and see!"

She lifted the gray gown from the couch and held it against her mother's little body; kissed the startled face that peered above it with tired, faded blue eyes.

"What *is* it?" her mother demanded.

"Mother," said Hilda, "I never knew you to be slow before. It's my wedding dress, of course—the wedding dress you're going to wear for me. And all that"—she waved toward the bedroom as well—"all that is our trousseau, Mother, yours and mine."

Mrs. Trask suddenly began to cry, her body shaking, and the tears rolling unchecked down her face. "I—I wanted you to have six of everything!" she wept, "and now you've got just a skimpy outfit after all."

"It's not skimpy!" Hilda denied. "And if it is skimpy, I don't care a single bit, and neither does Stan." The words were brave, but her eyes searched Stanley's face a bit tremulously: "You don't care," she challenged him, "do you, Stan?"

Stanley had watched the feminine proceedings, his expression clouded with a tender bewilderment that had lightened gradually into a tenderer comprehension. Now he shook off his role of silent spectator. Hilda was holding her mother close, but that did not deter him. He encircled them both with a mighty sweep of arms before he stopped to answer.

"My Perfectly Beautiful!" he whispered in Hilda's ear. And then, aloud, "You know I wouldn't care if it was skimpy. But this trousseau—why, Hilda, I'm proud of it as can be. I'm sure there *never* was another trousseau built for two ladies at once—*never* before!"

FLORENCE CRANNELL MEANS *was born in Baldwinsville, New York, in 1891. She wrote prolifically for family and children's magazines as well as writing many full-length works of fiction, primarily in the first half of the twentieth century.*

158 SPRUCE STREET

Author Unknown

The analysis of Mary MacGuire's piano-playing skill: "Sight-reading—excellent; fingering—good; touch—poor, stiff wrists." The two women in charge of recruiting new students headed to Mary's house to see if they could learn more.

———

A friend of young people in a certain city had made available a fund which would pay the expenses of ten selected students who showed outstanding musical talent, for a year of intensive study in a leading conservatory in the United States and two years following in Paris.

The slight girl who stood before the desk of the kindly woman in charge of one of the smaller schools whose pupils were eligible for the award, flushed with embarrassment. "I live at"—she hesitated—"1717 Massachusetts Avenue."

Mrs. Jackson looked up in surprise from the blank on which she had been recording the answers to certain routine questions required of all entrants. The girl had given her name and other information readily enough. She was Mary MacGuire, aged sixteen, and wished to enter as a beginner on the piano.

"Oh, won't you please let me study here?" she begged. "I'll work ever so hard."

"It means a lot to you, doesn't it," smiled Mrs. Jackson, "not only to work here with Madame Marche, but the possibility of being one of the Brandon appointees?"

"Oh, yes, I do want the scholarship so much!"

"I hope you will be successful," Mrs. Jackson was sympathetic, "but see this stack of applications. Mrs. Brandon picks the girls herself, you know, and there can only be ten.

"Let's see what the examiner says about your playing," and she turned to her record file. "Here it is: 'Sight-reading—excellent; fingering—good; touch'—now that is just too bad—'touch—poor, stiff wrists.'

"But never mind, my dear. Practice under Madam's instruction will soon rectify that if you're not afraid to work. We can do wonders for you in three months. And remember that not just musical ability counts. Mrs. Brandon puts a great deal of emphasis on personality. Don't look so tragic, my dear. I'll send our tuner out to limber up the action on your piano. That will help those stiff wrists."

"Please don't," the girl almost gasped. "I'd much rather have my piano fixed myself."

"But our men will understand just what is needed, and there'll be no charge. This service is free to our students."

The point that she was evidently to be accepted was lost to Mary for the moment. Her sensitive face was the picture of anxiety as she insisted that nobody be sent out to adjust her piano.

"What is wrong? Won't you tell me?" Mrs. Jackson put the

question gently, wondering in her own mind whether or not the girl was ashamed of her family—or of her home.

Mary's eyes flooded with tears, and for a moment she was silent. Then she looked up frankly. "I didn't give you my right address. I really live at 158 Spruce Street. But I didn't try to mislead you because I'm ashamed of my home or of my mother, who is a widow and works hard every day. We are very poor, and our home isn't much. But if you wish to meet my mother, I'll be glad to bring her here to your office someday."

Mrs. Jackson didn't press the matter, but she wondered.

The very next day Mrs. Brandon came in to look over the scholarship questionnaires. With the experience still fresh in her mind, Mrs. Jackson described her interview with Mary MacGuire, and voiced her question as to the why for the wrong address.

"We must find out about this girl right away," said Mrs. Brandon. "Let's go out this afternoon and explore 158 Spruce Street."

They found the house—and it was a poor little house. When the door opened a motherly little woman greeted them.

"Sure, an' Mary MacGuire lives here," she answered to their query.

"And ye be her music teachers? Come right in."

The tiny "front room" they entered was neat, but almost bare of furniture. Both visitors perched on a slippery haircloth sofa and looked about for the piano while Mrs. MacGuire spoke of her daughter proudly.

"I'll call her. She'll be that glad to see you! She talks about nothin' under hiven but her music, an' studyin' at the big conservative, an' goin' to Paris."

But Mary, when she was called, did not appear, and her mother finally pushed open the door into the kitchen, saying:

"Wheriver is the girl? I'll just see now?"

And an instant later she returned:

"Won't the both of ye come out here for a minute? It does beat all where she has gone to, but while she's away, I want ye to see what a smart child she is."

As the visitors stepped into the spotless kitchen, they noticed that the back door stood ajar, suggesting Mary's hasty exit.

"Ye see," her mother went on, "she's that skeered ye'll find out about—"

At that instant there was a step on the threshold, and a sobbing Mary came slowly toward the little group. "Oh, Mother," she said when she could speak, "Now they'll never, never choose me."

"There, there," comforted Mrs. MacGuire, as she hugged the weeping girl close, and pointed toward the window. There the guests saw an ironing board—just a common ironing board—with one end resting on the sill, and the other on a chair. It was upside down, and along the edge was pasted a piano chart.

"Me Mary dipped square spring clothes pins into ink and nailed them on," explained the proud mother, "to give her the feel of the black keys. Ain't she the smartest child in the town now?"

The visitors looked, and looked again in amazement. And then they began to question the MacGuires. The girl had never touched a real instrument, save an old organ that had belonged to a neighbor long since moved away. She had never had a real lesson. But she had perfected her sight-reading to excellent, her fingering to good, and got as far as possible with her touch—all on the underside of her mother's ironing board!

ALONG CAME CYNTHIA

Harriet Lummis Smith

The world is divided into two classes: Doers and Drones. Cynthia was the former, Blair the latter. And he liked his condition—until he walked into Cynthia's bare house. True, they were both victims of the terrible Depression, but their responses were totally different.

Life was not so bad, Blair reflected, when once a fellow accepted the fact that he was down and out. Defeat was not so bad. The unavailing struggle, the bitterness of disappointment were the intolerable factors.

He had graduated with a self-confidence based on a successful school life. He had done well in his studies, had acquitted himself with credit in athletics, and had won first prize in the senior essay contest. When he took his diploma, it never had occurred to him that these successes would not be duplicated immediately.

Finding a job had proved an incredibly difficult task; and when he finally *did* secure a position, it lasted only a month. The firm failed, owing him three weeks' salary. He needed the money, of course, but the more serious loss was the decrease of his self-confidence. When, after another two months, he secured a second position, he had a feeling that it wouldn't last either. As a matter of fact, it didn't. By this time Blair distrusted not only himself, but the world he lived in.

His bequest from his great-aunt seemed to him a piece of good fortune, although perhaps there was ground for a difference of opinion. The money was not left him outright, but the interest was to be paid him monthly as long as he lived. The principal was then to be turned over to an Old People's Home. During his lifetime, however, Blair would have twenty-five dollars a month between him and need.

At first he thought of the money as a stopgap. It would help him out until he had secured another job. Since he was practically penniless, however, he realized the need of living very simply until he was again earning. He found a cheap little room in the third story of a shabby house which he rented for a dollar and a quarter a week, with the privilege of preparing his own meals.

That first summer he got along comfortably. An observer might have noticed that he didn't rise so early as formerly to pursue his search for work, and that he quit earlier in the afternoon. It was pleasant in the park these summer days, much pleasanter than down in the business section of the city.

Cold weather came, and Blair adapted himself to the change. It was surprising how much cooking one could do on a one-burner gas stove. Cornmeal mush and oatmeal were both cheap and filling. The park was no longer attractive as a lounging place, but he found in the city library a satisfactory substitute. He spent a number of hours there every day. The library reading-room was much pleasanter than the city streets, especially in bad weather. Blair fell into the habit of looking through the newspaper want advertise-

ments and answering those which seemed promising. Naturally, they were not numerous.

By the end of the first year Blair had discovered that he could live on twenty-five dollars a month. After the second winter he reached the comfortable conclusion that to be down-and-out was as good as anything else if a fellow didn't make a fuss about it. He didn't fuss. The fiction he read in such quantities was almost like a drug. He lived in a world of unreality, his only friends, his books. For some time he had been invited to the homes of acquaintances, but the invitations had gradually become fewer and by now had practically ceased. He had given up church because he couldn't budget twenty-five dollars a month and allow for anything to put on the plate.

One March day Blair left the library about four o'clock. He had read an entire book at one sitting and the windy outdoor world seemed less real than what he had just left. He crossed the street, proceeding on his way, when a voice called his name: "Blair!"

Blair stopped jerkily. A girl was coming toward him, her face aglow. As she drew nearer, an expression of uncertainty showed for a moment. "You *are* Blair Kingsley, aren't you? Why, of *course* you are."

"Cynthia!" he gasped. He hadn't seen Cynthia Hunt since they both were high school students. When the Hunts had gone West, hoping to find a climate where Mr. Hunt wouldn't suffer from asthma, Cynthia and he had agreed to write often. They had done so, indeed, for several months, and then their letters had become more and more infrequent, finally ceasing altogether. He saw with a little thrill that Cynthia was better looking, that she carried herself extremely well, and that she showed a pleasure over meeting him that had become a rarity in his experience.

He walked along beside her, listening to her explanations of her efforts to locate him. "I asked Nell and Robin and Carlotta about you, and none of them could tell me a thing. Said they hadn't seen you for ages."

"You can't be more surprised to see me than I am to see you," he returned. "How long have you been back? Have you come to stay?"

"Yes, to stay. You knew Father died, didn't you? Six months

ago, and we just waited till our tenants' lease was up and then we came back."

"To the old home, you mean?" Blair spoke rather incredulously. He had known that old house very well. It was hard to think of it as again occupied by the Hunts.

"Yes, we're at number 730 again. It's terribly battered after five years of tenants, but after all, it's home."

He walked on beside her, trying to find an excuse for saying good-bye. For the first time in a year he was conscious of the shabbiness of his clothes; but Cynthia was talking as though she didn't notice that his coat was threadbare and his shoes patched. She had a job, it seemed, not as good job as she might wish for, but distinctly better than nothing. "What are *you* doing?" she asked.

"Well, I'm not doing anything just at present."

She made no comment but began to tell him of some of her interesting experiences in the West. Finally, when they reached the house, she said cordially, "Come in and say hello to Mother, won't you, Blair?"

"Oh, I can't tonight, Cynthia. Some—some other time."

"All right," she agreed pleasantly. "I'm likely to be home evenings, Blair, till we're really settled, so come soon. Mother has kept asking about you."

She went up the steps, and he turned away quickly. He had not been so upset for many a month. Just as he was becoming accustomed to doing nothing and living on next to nothing, along came Cynthia. He was suddenly aware of everything he lacked, of his shabby clothes and his empty pockets. He felt bruised as though he'd been in a fight. Well, the remedy was simple. He would keep out of Cynthia's way.

Two evenings later he called at Cynthia's home, and Mrs. Hunt came to the door. She looked at him kindly, but without recognition. "I'm afraid—" she began.

"Good evening, Mrs. Hunt," he said, taking off his hat. "I'm Blair Kingsley."

"Oh, Blair!" she cried. "Come right in. Cynthia is—dear me, Cynthia, I told you you shouldn't do that work tonight."

"Come in, Blair," called a cheerful voice. Blair approached the door of the large room to the right of the hall. It was empty of furniture, and Cynthia was sitting on the floor holding a piece of sandpaper. "I'm getting this floor in shape," she announced casually. "It's a good hardwood floor, Blair, and after it's been scraped down and shined up, it'll look like new."

"Can I—can I help you?" asked Blair. He spoke without enthusiasm, but she accepted heartily.

"Of course you can. Go and hang your coat and hat on the rack in the hall, and take a cushion off the couch there, to protect your knees. I've enough sandpaper for both of us."

She had. It was half past ten before they stopped work, and although the evening's activities had been a postscript to a day's work for Cynthia, she seemed as fresh as a lark. Blair, who hadn't done a day's work for two years, was at the point of exhaustion.

"All this stimulates the appetite," said Cynthia. "Let's go into the kitchen and have some cocoa and sandwiches. How about you, Mummy? Hungry?"

While she made the cocoa and sliced bread for the sandwiches, Cynthia enlightened Blair as to her plans for the kitchen. "I'm going to paint everything white. Mother has to spend so much of her time here that the least I can do is to make it pretty."

The sandwiches and cocoa made the most appetizing meal Blair had tasted for months. He stopped eating after a while because he was afraid Cynthia would guess how much he was enjoying it. The walk to his own quarters was a long one, but although it was past midnight when he reached his room and he was lame from head to foot from his unaccustomed exertions, he didn't go to sleep readily. Strange how dissatisfied he felt after renewing his acquaintance with Cynthia. He had assumed he was over wanting things, and now, it seemed to him that he wanted everything. *If I'm sensible, I'll keep away from that girl,* he reflected angrily.

On Saturday afternoon when he told himself that he would walk by the house, but not go in, perhaps he meant to stick to that resolution. He had not counted on discovering Cynthia in her own back yard, with a spade leaning against the fence and pruning shears in her hand. He had no sooner discovered her than she discovered him, and beckoned him to join her. "I'm trimming up this rose," she said. "It used to be beautiful. It's a shame the way the tenants neglected it."

"Looks to me as though it were dead," Blair announced. "Guess you're wasting your time."

"Appearances are deceitful," Cynthia reminded him. "I'm going to give it a chance, anyway." She snipped away the dead branches with energy. Before long Blair was using the spade, under her direction.

A man in the next yard watched him for a time and then came to the fence. "I say, young fellow."

Blair straightened himself, staring, and the man went on, "I want somebody to do the same sort of work you're doing for Mrs. Hunt. What day next week could you give me?"

Blair started to explain that there was some mistake; then he glanced at Cynthia. Nothing in her expression indicated that she thought her neighbor's blunder amusing. Blair heard himself saying, "I'm not a gardener, but I can obey orders. And I can come any day."

"Then we'll say Monday. My wife will boss the job. She would, anyway, if you were the best gardener to be had."

So Blair Kingsley got his first job in two years. Cynthia made no comment. After a time she looked at her wrist watch and said, "Let's go in and wash up, Blair. It's almost time for supper."

The attendants at the library must have wondered what had become of Blair, for the next few weeks were perhaps the most strenuous of his life. The wife of the man who had engaged him for a day's work in the garden was pleased with him and kept him nearly a week. Other housewives offered him employment. He beat rugs, washed windows, cleaned cellars, and spaded flower beds. Frequently, after a hard day's work, he came to Cynthia's in the evening to help her with her campaign of renovation. Cynthia was tireless herself and seemed to take it for granted that he was the same.

When the check for twenty-five dollars arrived the latter part of the month, Blair was not out of money as usual. Not only had his days of toil been reasonably profitable, but his employers had always supplied him with a meal, sometimes two. Looking at the twenty-five dollar check, Blair reached a sudden astonishing conclusion. The next day he went about looking for the places where clothing could be bought cheaply, and purchased socks, shirts, and underwear. The next day he bought shoes, a marked-down suit that cost him only fifteen dollars, a hat, and two neckties.

When he awoke the morning after that orgy of spending, he realized that it was the first of May. It was not one of those bleak and blustery May days which seem to take pleasure in belying their reputations, but was warm and lovely. Blair had a job that morning helping a wrecking crew that was tearing down an old house in the neighborhood. It was a disagreeable job, with plaster flying, nails projecting threateningly, and big rafters slipping, but he stuck to it grimly until six o'clock. When he received his pay, he was told that he could report the next day if he wished to. The pay was more generous than he had yet received, and he went home feeling almost wealthy.

After a hasty meal he donned his new clothes, and set out in Cynthia's direction. Cynthia was in the back yard, of course, making the most of the daylight. She looked up and gazed at him blankly. When she recognized him, the color deepened in her cheeks, but all she said was, "Come in, Blair. I want to show you something."

The rose bush he had pronounced dead was putting out green leaves. Cynthia pointed them out, her voice tremulous with pride. "I told you I was going to give it a chance, and now see!"

Blair stood looking. Those infinitesimal specks of green seemed to him symbols of that which was happening to himself. After months when life seemed static, when hopes and desires were quiescent, he felt the stirring of new ambition, new longing. After his years of discouragement and failure, somehow he felt sure that success was just ahead.

HARRIET LUMMIS SMITH (?–1947) *born in Auburndale, Massachusetts, was a prolific writer of inspirational and value-based stories early in the twentieth century. Besides writing books such as* Other People's Business *(1916), she wrote the three books in the* Peggy Raymond *series and the four later books in the* Pollyanna *series (1924–1929), as well as a large number of short stories.*

MY SON—HANDICAPPED

Author Unknown

How does a parent face crippling illness in her child? How much should the child be protected from hurt in the future?

How is a parent to know?

This story is an old one, a fact to be kept in mind when medical costs are mentioned.

I tucked my five-year-old son into bed after a gay day of romping on the beach. He gave me a kiss, and I slipped away, full of the joy that his health gave to me.

Infantile paralysis struck that night. For months my son's tortured limbs lay in cotton packs. Only fragments of memories of those days survive, happily. But there was one evening when my husband and I sat beside Larry's bed and heard the doctor say that he would live. His little old man's face lolled grotesquely from a neck powerless to support it on his wasted body. Could this be my glowing, frolicking son of the beach?

That was sixteen years ago. Larry is still a cripple. But—

Only a few weeks ago, Larry walked into the living room and

draped a sweater with its big varsity letter over an easy chair. At the same time he brought the news that he had won another scholarship; one that will enable him to go onward into medical school.

This is the story of the how of it all came to pass. There was no miracle, and there will be none. My son's right leg is still three inches shorter than the left, the thigh no bigger around than your wrist. He yanks it along with a powerful right arm when he walks, and he will always have to do this.

But in spite of what is called his handicap, Larry's record of achievement today classes him as an above-the-average college senior. More important by far, Larry knows himself to be a whole man among men. No brooding introspection plagues him.

Soon after that unforgettable night sixteen years ago, my husband and I faced our problem. We would teach Larry to build a full, valuable life. We told each other that to do this he must give all he could to the world, rather than take all that people rushed to hand him.

We picked the hard way—for ourselves as well as for Larry. It would have been much easier to have babied him, shielded him. That was what I longed to do. But I determined that I would not.

Of course, for months after infantile paralysis struck, all my husband and I could do was to preserve life itself. Six months after the attack, however, Larry began to move his head a little. I began a regime calculated by doctors to give him the maximum opportunity for development; though there was no promise of any progress whatever. After Larry's breakfast, I gave him a bath in salt water imported from the sea. A thorough liniment rub, massaging of the legs and feet, and an endless hour of exercising them by flexing followed. Then a rest period, lunch, and an hour outdoors in the wheelchair.

Larry could not leave his chair, but he could throw a rubber

ball for Fritz, our police dog, to fetch. We managed to train Fritz not to release the ball until Larry leaned slightly from his chair and took it from the dog's mouth. A trifling thing, but for all that, a beginning in doing for himself.

My husband had been a rather famous college athlete, and he saw to it that Larry used all that was not impaired in as much sport as possible. He bought Larry a small rifle. Together, as intense as any experts in Olympic competition, they sat on the back porch and fired in turn at bottles. Scores were kept week by week, and no golfer was ever more jealous of his score than Larry of his. This practice made Larry the best of all the boys in the neighborhood later on.

We also gave Larry duties as early as possible, and the first of them came naturally. Before infantile paralysis struck, it was his pleasure to hold my chair and slide it beneath me at dinner, with comic courtliness. He could no longer do that. But he could reach out from his wheelchair and hand me a napkin. Each evening he did so, with the same comic courtliness. Once more a trifling thing, but a beginning in doing for others.

My husband and I had to venture into the unknown with our program, and there were times when I trembled with the fear that I was being an inhuman mother. The summer after the stroke, we decided to take Larry to our seaside cottage again—the scene of the attack. I mentioned it casually. His eyes grew wide with terror. "Mother, not *there!*" he begged. "Something will happen to me again if we go there."

My heart simply dissolved inside me. Assurances that he need never again go to our beach cottage rushed to my lips. But I shut them tight. If I had let Larry be conquered by his fear of the place, I would have betrayed him. When I could control my speech I said:

"Larry, you must come along with us this summer. Nothing will happen ever again at the cottage. If you're not happy, I'll bring you straight back home. But you must try it."

On the way to the seaside, Larry was so disturbed he couldn't eat. We hustled him into his swimming suit when we arrived, and my husband carried him into the sea, piggyback. He floated, supported by my husband's hand. He grinned. In less than an hour he was as happy a beachcomber as he ever had been.

Two entirely unnecessary operations, designed to transplant muscles and lengthen the Achilles tendon, delayed any attempt to place Larry in school. If they were unnecessary, why did we submit our tortured child to them? Because of the word *maybe*—a word I have grown to hate. Maybe, we were told, the operations would restore independent locomotion to our son's legs. We felt we dared not deny Larry the chance. Both operations—one when he was six, and another nine months later—did nothing except give him added pain and more mental hazards.

The problem of discipline was hardest of all for me, in those early years. When Larry was eight, we were able to take him to a small private school each morning. My son showed no more passionate enthusiasm for regular study than the average boy. Mutinies were frequent. One came while a woman friend was visiting me.

"I don't want to study, and I'm not going to study," Larry announced. Persuasion failed. I took him over my knee and gave him a good spanking. I noticed my friend grew white. She left shortly after.

"I never believed I'd think the same of you after I saw you whack that poor child in those braces," she told me recently. "Now, when I see Larry, I understand."

At the age of nine, we entered Larry in grammar school. He wore braces on both legs at the time, and he got around with crutches and, later, canes. He did very well with them but, naturally, he could not keep pace with his schoolmates.

"Oh, Mother, if I could only run!" he pleaded one day when he came home exhausted. All we could do to help was to substitute every activity possible for the running that was impossible. My husband taught Larry to swim very well for his age. We turned our yard into a neighborhood playground, and our house into a playhouse.

There was nothing synthetic about Larry's participation in the baseball and football games in our backyard. At first, the other boys wanted to substitute somebody to run for him. He didn't approve. He did his own batting and his own running—hopping around the bases for dear life on his good left leg. In football he took his own bumps. Often I stood watching from the window. Time and again Larry fell heavily, his braces twisted beneath him. Time and again I ran to help him, my stomach turning over inside me with fear that he had hurt himself seriously. Time and again I caught myself on the threshold, while Larry was hauled, laughing to his feet.

Of course there were joyous surprises, too. At eleven, we first sent Larry to a camp. Thereafter he went every summer for six years, won a table-load of cups in swimming races, and finally served as counselor.

The years took wing after Larry's eleventh. He won honors in scholarship in high school, and was class president and editor of the school paper. He took his lumps on the athletic field, too. He not only managed the football team but, after he was able to discard crutches and canes, pitched for the junior varsity in baseball.

It was about this time that I realized Larry was missing something in social life. I suggested that he join his friends at one of their dances.

"Mother, that's too much," he said. "They won't want me. I could only sit around like a bump on a log."

I felt that I couldn't take this refusal without depriving Larry of a part of life. He had no sisters and brothers, and needed social life.

A girl in our neighborhood was inordinately shy. She invariably became tongue-tied in the presence of young men. Larry and I had discussed this. One evening, as though the idea had just struck me, I said: "I've been thinking that we ought to try to help Sue. Why don't we give a party and ask her? She'll feel at home here, and if you pay a lot of attention to her, Larry, maybe she'll get used to it and forget about herself."

"She'll be so bored she'll be driven into other society, eh?" said Larry.

But the idea clicked. We gave the party. Larry, as host, paid extraordinary attention to Sue. This took him away from the piano, his usual post at such parties in the home.

I forgot to mention that, when he was a youngster, I decided on the piano as a social wedge for my son. The only teacher available was an elderly musician committed to a respectful approach to the classics. Larry balked bitterly at practice. I finally persuaded the teacher into a livelier attack on music, with such numbers as "I Can't Give You Anything But Love." This reconciled Larry to the piano.

As the party's pace accelerated, Larry became so interested in the problem, really a lovely little bud, that he forgot about everything else. Sue had refused several dance invitations from others. Larry took her to task in the flippant, chivalrous vernacular of the day, and before he knew it they were on the dance floor. They giggled and danced. One dance led to another, and Larry has been dancing ever since—not expertly, but enthusiastically.

In his sophomore year at high school, Larry was forced to face another crisis. A surgeon thought that a new operation might free him from the brace on his left leg. But Larry refused to undergo the operation. The decision was motivated by the most powerful influence in the world—the fear of pain.

I have not described the endless tortures that had been inflicted on my son, but I must recount one incident to make clear his state of mind at this time. I was told that a boy in the slums who was suffering from progressive infantile paralysis might be helped by a transfusion of Larry's blood.

"No," I said at once. I could not endure more pain for Larry.

"Think it over," said the surgeon. He gave me a strange look.

I could not bear thinking it over. I told Larry.

"Oh, Mother, I can't, I just can't," he said.

I said no more. Two or three days later Larry came to me and said: "Mother, I've been thinking about that boy. And how can I say no? I'll have the transfusion whenever they want. Will it hurt, Mother?"

There was terror of pain in my son's words. I cannot describe the fury I felt at that moment—fury at those who had suggested that my son be tortured because "maybe" it might help someone he had never seen.

The transfusion hurt. It increased Larry's fear of pain. It helped to create the state of mind that resulted in his opposition to the operation the surgeon counseled. The surgeon was anxious to perform the operation. But he said, "We owe Larry the right to answer for himself now," and we dropped the subject.

A year later Larry said to me: "Mother, I want that operation on my left leg. If I don't have it, I know I'll never be satisfied."

The operation was completely successful. While Larry lay with his leg in a plaster cast for ten weeks, friends and classmates flocked to his room. One of the happiest days of my life came when the cast was taken from his leg and he took a step on it. He blew a kiss to his just covered brace and laughed. The face of the surgeon was alight.

Fortunately, Larry's scholastic record won him a university scholarship. Without it, college would have been impossible. Our family fortunes were all misfortunes, from the day the Depression began, and we could not have paid tuition at the Pacific Coast university that he attended. I want to note here that if we had not been in rather comfortable circumstances during Larry's childhood, I doubt whether we could have carried through our course. The first year of Larry's illness cost us $3,000, and for a long time, medical and massage expenses averaged $150 monthly.

During his first year at college, Larry, for the first time, felt that a barrier held him apart from the life of other young men. His first months were painful. Every freshman finds, with a shock, that he is not the hail-fellow-well-met that he was as a high-school senior. The collegiate social system is designed to humiliate him. Larry's affliction, exhibited in an alien environment, was suddenly magnified. He wrote me that he saw little of his classmates. True, he was working toward a place on one of the college publications, but he was shut off from the easy fellowship of the athletic field and locker rooms. He missed athletics.

I consulted my friend, the surgeon. Though there would be some risk, he thought Larry might go out for gymnastic work requiring shoulder strength rather than pedal agility. Larry went out for the gym team, and the coach, discovering his powerful shoulder development, tried him out at two major gymnastic events. Larry practiced as faithfully as any freshman fullback. He injured his left leg severely—so severely that a new kind of brace had to be devised for use in one of the events. But he kept on. Larry not only made the team, he eventually won the intercollegiate championships in his two events. More than that, he was now one of the boys in the locker room. He had climbed the barrier.

One night last summer when my son was home on vacation I could not help asking, "Larry, do you think you're handicapped?"

"No, I don't, Mother," he answered. "I've had one advantage since I was sick, and I still have it: I don't like to have people do things for me. That's an advantage."

I believe, with Larry, that a very real handicap may provide its own compensations. But I also know that not every mother can give a child the attention that I gave Larry. If I had had other children, I should have been forced to neglect either them or Larry.

All in all, though, I'm sure that what Larry did is, to some degree, possible for a large number of handicapped boys and girls. Larry is equally sure of this. For he is going to be an orthopedic surgeon. He feels that he can thus give to others what he has given to himself, and in so giving, find happiness.

HER INSIDE FACE

Beth Bradford Gilchrist

This old story is set in a time prior to the existence of today's near miraculous plastic surgery techniques—once you realize that bleak reality, the story takes on an entirely different dimension.

Bob Armstrong did not like girls. And Bob Armstrong was not himself an unlikable fellow. He liked his sister Nan, of course, but Nan's friends often bored him. "Nothing but pretty faces without anything behind them," he said. "Silly and giggly and useless. For friendship, better stick to your own kind. A girl has nothing to offer, unless you want to do girly sort of things." And Bob most distinctly didn't care for that sort of thing. He liked a good pal and the things you did with a good pal. Who ever found such fellowship with a girl? Except Nan. She was all right. If Nan had gone to a different school, perhaps—Nan's friends were all girls from her school. Bob didn't think much of that school. He told Father so.

Nan was aware that Bob didn't care for the girls she brought home. "You don't know them," she argued.

"Don't care to," said Bob. "They're not worth knowing."

But he was polite. Bob had manners. And the girls who visited Nan never knew how Bob felt about them. They all liked Bob—liked him immensely—and tagged around after him like a flock of sheep, whenever Bob didn't escape before they saw him.

———————

At spring vacation of her last year Nan came home full of a new girl. Jane—Jane—Jane. Nan's tongue fairly dripped Janes.

"You'd like Jane, Bob," said Nan. "She's different."

"How?" asked Bob.

"Independent," said Nan. "And jolly and friendly, and quiet too, and she likes people immensely, and books, and she's one of the best students, and she just loves out of doors, and—oh, I never saw any girl like her."

"I've heard that before."

"It's so this time," Nan insisted earnestly.

"Every other month you pick up a new topnotcher."

"Not like Jane. But I can't describe her. I never knew anybody with her combination of qualities. The girls all admire and love her."

That was no recommendation to Bob.

"Pretty?"

"Yes, indeed."

"A grind, you say?"

"Not a grind. But she's good in class. She likes to know things for the sake of knowing them. Not just to get by."

"Huh!" said Bob. He doubted it. He felt that he had seen too many of Nan's enthusiasms to take them at their face value.

Nan stood on the hearth rug and surveyed Bob's lazy length on the couch.

"If you ever meet Jane," said Nan, "I'm sure you'll sit up and take notice, Bob Armstrong. She's the most amazing girl I ever saw. She's"—Nan groped for words—"she's so—so real."

Bob's eyes twinkled.

That exasperated Nan. "She won't turn over her hand to make you notice her."

Bob grinned. "Hurrah!"

"Now you're being horrid. But it's so. She likes girls just as well as she likes boys!"

"Don't believe it," said Bob calmly. "Lucky she's pretty. That's the only thing a girl's got."

"If I can get her up here next summer, I'll show you a girl with more than that." There was a threat in Nan's tone. "I wonder—maybe I can. Her father's a scientist, and he's off for the year in some out-of-the-world spot studying something odd. That's why she's at my school. Her people get home in September. I heard her say so."

"She'll come," declared Bob.

"I wish I were as sure as you. She's too popular, and it isn't, you see, as if she'd care for visiting us just because we live where we do. Oh, I've had girls accept invitations just for the sake of being able to talk about it afterward—'When I was at High Meredith with the Armstrongs last summer.'" Nan shrugged the sentence aside. "I'll have to work to get Jane Cameron."

Bob forgot all about it. When Nan wrote, "Jane can't come. She's going to an aunt's for most of the summer and all the rest of her time is promised," he dimly remembered.

When Nan jubilantly announced, "Such luck! One of the places Jane was going to is quarantined for something. And I've persuaded her to come to us instead," he was only mildly curious. Nan got these enthusiasms sometimes. He had seen her work through some odd ones.

Jane Cameron came. She came with four other girls from Nan's school. *Girls were as alike outside as peas in a pod,* thought Bob, as he was introduced to them at the station. They wore different colors, but their clothes had the same lines, their hair the same style cut, their ideas could be counted on to be shaped by an identical pattern. Nan's brother couldn't see that Nan's vaunted friend was other than a tall, slim, straight-nosed girl with a friendly handshake and a clear eye. But she made no attempt to sit beside the chauffeur. Without the slightest hesitation, she stepped into the tonneau beside Nan. Bob at the wheel, with a girl bubbling exclamations beside him and two or three more throwing remarks over his shoulder, was aware of a certain point of quietness at his back. Perhaps Jane Cameron wouldn't bother him, after all.

She didn't. It was astonishing, but she didn't. She took everything that came along as it came, and enjoyed it. She was as ready to play tennis with girls as with boys, and she let Doris Crane carry Bob off for a game while she played with twelve-year-old Curtis. She was as happy afterward as if she'd had Curt's more "grown-up" brother. And Curt adored her.

"Jane's a fine girl," he told Bob judiciously.

Really, Bob thought, *he could give her a better game.* He undertook to show her how good a game he could give her.

She was Nan's guest, wasn't she? Bob discovered his responsibilities. He must find out what had so captivated his sister.

He hadn't yet discovered to his satisfaction when the accident happened. Bob was at the wheel. But it was distinctly not his fault. The other driver was held responsible. Bob was exonerated, but that fact didn't mend that nice straight nose of Jane's. She was the only one in either car seriously hurt.

Jane was quite cool. "It's my nose," she said when they picked her up. *Obviously,* it was her nose. "Is there a hospital near?"

That remark showed, Nan said afterward, that Jane came of a scientific family.

Bob drove Nan and Jane and a woman from the other car to the hospital. Jane was the coolest of them all. When they got to the hospital, she refused to take a room.

"I'll go into a ward," said Jane.

"Give her the best room in the house," said Bob. "Father will wish it."

"No, please," said Jane, choking a little, but firm. "What would I do in a room all by myself? In a ward there'll be people to watch. I'll not be lonely. I prefer a ward."

Jane got her ward. She so obviously meant it. It seemed to comfort her. But it couldn't comfort Bob. After all, he'd been driving. And Jane's nose had been so nice and straight. Now—who knew what it would be?

"The doctor says the bone is crushed," Nan told the house party at home. "Not all the way. But some of it is gone. Isn't that awful?"

It *was* awful.

"She'll be disfigured for life," said Fay Eastman.

"Don't," wailed Nan.

"Maybe it won't be so bad as that," said Hope Devereaux, "but she certainly won't look the same."

"Jane's nose was her best feature too," pronounced Doris Crane.

"Oh, girls, it's too terrible! Scarred for life and in our house and our car and my own brother driving," mourned Nan.

"And Jane's such a darling!"

Bob was talking with his father. "There wasn't anything else to do, Father," said Bob. "I thought they'd miss us, but—well, they didn't." Bob's face looked gray. "She's a plucky thing. Not a whimper. And she made 'em put her in a ward. Said it would be company. Say, Father," the boy broke out, "why couldn't it have been *my* nose or my arm or something? A girl's face—"

"I know, son."

"I don't think she quite realizes it yet. I hung around till the doctors finished, and then I made Dr. Phelps tell me. Part of the bone's gone. There's bound to be some disfigurement. Phelps wouldn't talk much, but I figured that out."

"We'll do what we can, son."

It was an excited, unhappy household that went to bed at the Armstrongs'. Jane was so dear, so jolly, so plucky, everybody loved her so. And to have this come! Out of a clear sky, in the midst of such light-hearted happiness! A girl's face made such a difference. Talking couldn't alter the fact. *It did make a difference.*

How the girls felt was nothing to how Bob felt. Had not he been at the wheel? All night he stared into darkness. That he wasn't to blame didn't help much. A girl had been disfigured while he was driving. Why couldn't it have been *his* nose? Bob, without a "nerve" in his body, felt shaken, bewildered, apprehensive. You read in the papers of accidents. You knew, of course, that they might happen, but you didn't expect them to happen to *you*. Above all, you didn't expect to lose your nerve over them.

Bob had heard that engineers of fast trains were of no further use on a run after they'd been through an accident, even though it had been due to no fault of theirs. They had to be transferred to slower trains. Bob hadn't understood it. He'd been sure he wouldn't lose his nerve. And now—well, now he knew how they felt. He couldn't forget how Jane had looked. He saw her—before and after. No, Bob didn't sleep much.

In the morning, the telephone reported that Jane had passed "a comfortable night."

"I'm going over," said Nan, "the first thing. It won't hurt her to have us, if she can stand the ward. But we can't all go at once. Bob and I go first. It's our right. I can read to her. And we can plan relays so she'll never be lonesome during visiting hours. Funny of Jane to choose a ward. But that's just like her. You never can tell what she's going to do. And she does like people. You girls can go over later."

"I'll do it for Jane," said Doris Crane heroically. "But I'd rather do most anything else! I can't bear to see disfigured people. And I know I shall cry!"

"Then you can just stay at home," said Nan.

"No, I'm going, because it's Jane."

"Not if you cry."

Nan was adamant.

"Then I won't. But, oh, dear, I'll want to."

———

Bob drove Nan over. His face was white, his eyes heavy, and he drove as slowly as Great Aunt Susan. Nan didn't mention the fact, but she noticed it. She also saw that Bob hated to go in.

"You needn't, if you don't want to."

"I'm going," said Bob. His lips were set grimly.

Nan and Bob, laden with fruit, books, and all the delicacies and alleviations concerned minds could suggest, walked into the ward.

Jane was laughing. It was a perfectly natural light-hearted sound. You couldn't see much of her face, it was so covered with bandages, but her eyes peeped out and her tongue was busy. On one side of her was an Italian girl with a broken leg, on the other a child with a twisted back. The ward babbled with languages.

Jane greeted her visitors merrily and introduced them right and left.

"Isn't it lucky it's nothing worse than my nose? It would be dreadful if I couldn't talk a mile a minute! Peaches! How delightful! And such beauties. Won't we feast, 'Nita? Pass them round, Bob. Look over those books, Ruth. Take them to her, somebody. You may find something interesting. I'm sorry, Nan, to have upset your house party, but it's very interesting here, really. What are you all doing today?"

There wasn't any chance to say any of the things they'd come to say. There wasn't a chance to say how sorry they were or to commiserate with Jane at all, Jane herself was so full of talk about the people she had just come to know.

Nan did say, "Everything's going to be done for you that can be done."

And Jane said, "Oh, yes, your father and mother were over last night and they saw to everything. They're dears, Nan."

Then she looked up at Bob out of her bandaged face. "Bob, you're to stop thinking you're in the least responsible, because you're not. It's as plain as day nobody in our car was to blame."

"We've been feeling terribly, Jane," said Nan, "because it's your face."

"Part of my nose seems to be gone," said Jane serenely. "I'm sorry, too. But beauty comes from inside, you know. It's your character. So it doesn't do much harm to have a crooked nose, if you haven't a crooked soul. *A motor car can't smash my inside face. If that's broken, it's my own doing!*"

Jane meant it. She spoke quite serenely, and exactly as if she had been discussing something you could see. There wasn't the least hypocrisy or cant or self-consciousness about it. Jane was too matter-of-fact for that.

"Jane," said Nan, "you darling! I'm going to kiss you."

"That's nice," said Jane. "But what for?"

"Your soul, I think," said Nan. And she kissed her.

Bob felt something heavy and unhappy and hard roll off his shoulders. All at once he felt light and free, as if he'd been shut away in a dark, cold prison and now was out again in the sunshine. He had never before known such a feeling of release, as he had never before known such an anxiety to be freed from. The odd part was, everything was exactly as it had been before he walked into that ward. Not a thing had changed, not even the cause of his apprehension. Yet it was gone. Jane had banished it, Jane, laughing out of her bandages—friendly, matter-of-fact Jane.

Bob didn't say much of anything. He only looked at Jane. He passed the peaches to her new friends, and he brought and carried books for her, and he did everything he could find to do. When Nan got ready to go, Bob lingered a minute. He held out his hand, and Jane put her fingers in it and gave him a warm, firm grip. And Bob said words he hadn't the least notion he was going to say, words he had never thought of.

"Bless you, Jane," was what he said.

Then he drove home almost at his normal speed. His color was better, and he seemed, Nan noticed, much more like his usual self.

"Didn't I tell you Jane was the real thing?"

"You did," said Bob.

"It's going to be a pity, though, about her face."

"A pity about—" Bob stared. "Oh, her face! What difference does the shape of her nose make in a girl like that?"

"That's all right to say now, when we're all so relieved that Jane's feeling as she does about it. But when the excitement is over and her nose is spoiled and her face scarred, for just as long as she lives—you've got to think of that," argued Nan.

"She'll have her 'character.'" Bob's mouth drew into a queer little grin.

"Oh, Jane's amazing," Nan acknowledged. "But I wonder— Bob, my character isn't lovely enough to make up for a crushed nose."

Bob swung the car around a corner before he spoke. Then all he said was, "Jane's is."

"You seem," said his sister demurely, "to have changed your mind about the girls at my school. I thought you said none of 'em could possibly be worth knowing."

"There seems to be one that is," answered Bob, "and what's more, I'm going to know her."

BETH BRADFORD GILCHRIST (1879–1957) *was born in Peacham, Vermont. She was a prolific short-story writer, being published in many family and literary magazines, as well as writing the Helen series for girls. During the first quarter of the twentieth century she was at her peak of productivity and popularity.*

THE DISSOLVING
OF A PARTNERSHIP

Abbie Farwell Brown

It was to be an ideal marriage: a genuine partnership with each pursuing separate careers. Then came the terrible accident, with consequences unimaginable—he would be blind for the rest of his life.

It seemed…best to dissolve the partnership.

This story is almost a century old, but its message is a contemporary one. At the time it was written, two-career families were rare.

It was toward evening of an April day, beautiful with the forwardness of a suburban spring, when Julia ran briskly up the steps and let herself into the house with a shout of triumph.

"Ho, Mother! I have it!" she cried up the stairs. "And I shall be famous yet. I can almost see my name in red letters on big yellow posters all over the city— *Julia Royce, the great Pianiste*—"

She stopped suddenly, frightened by the expression on the face of her mother, who was coming down to meet her.

"Hush, dear," said the latter gravely. "I am sorry to chill your triumph so. It's as much to me as to you. But—something very dreadful has happened, and we must be quiet here in the house."

Julia's face blanched. "It's not David?" she said quickly. "Is he dead, Mother?"

"No, not dead, but very badly hurt, dear. He is upstairs in your room."

"Oh, what was it—tell me!" gasped the girl, falling into a chair helplessly.

"There was an accident to the train just outside the station here, two hours ago—strange you heard nothing of it as you came in. Several persons were killed. David was coming here, I suppose. The doctor recognized him and had him brought to us. They're working over him now."

"Do they think—he'll die?" Julia asked almost in a whisper.

"They cannot tell, he's so cut and shattered; they hope he may pull through. But they fear for his eyes, at best. Oh, my dear, if he should be blind!"

Julia staggered to her room. David near to death—who was so full of life and buoyant spirits. David shattered and maimed—who was so strong and handsome; with so much to live for and so much to do; with only a few of his books yet written, yet the public clamoring for more. With all those waiting note-books of plots and plans, and all that eager brain full of noble ideas and sweet imaginings. It was too cruel!

Only the night before they had been planning together for the future, pooling their ambitions, as it were, and confident of success. Each had so much to do before and after their marriage. If his next book were as successful as the last they would spend their honeymoon abroad, returning to meet the concert engagements which she confidently expected for the fall. For they had agreed to

follow out each his career so promisingly begun, and not to let marriage of true minds admit impediments to an individual ambition. It was to be a partnership of two independent firms; not—as Julia scornfully spoke of several schoolmates' marriages—the swallowing up of an excellent small shop by one of the monster department stores.

Julia took herself and her art very seriously. Her music master, who was very much in love with her, believed her to be a prodigy. People who had heard her play were dazzled by her youth and magnetism and were pleased to make much of her. She was the latest pretty girl to make a concert debut, and was the season's fad until a newer sensation should appear. Everyone, even David, flattered her; not realizing the unkindness and injustice they were doing to her. Who ever feels responsible in the matter of encouraging or of not encouraging striving young enthusiasm?

For days there was an awful stillness in the house. People went about on tiptoe and spoke in whispers, for David's life still hung in the balance, and no one saw him but the doctors and the nurse. The piano stood mute, as if sharing the general anxiety. Julia had no heart to practice during those first days of suspense; but her mother, wiser in the medicine for sorrow, and even with an eye to her daughter's ambition, at last came forward and peremptorily insisted that she should keep her mind occupied and her fingers limber. She was a kindly woman, but withal a practical one, to whom Julia owed a large part of her ambition, and even in a crisis like the present one, she never lost sight of the goal which she had set for her daughter.

After some days of listless inexertion, in sheer desperation Julia decided to visit a neighbor's home and borrow the use of her piano. And thereafter she filled her usual hours of practice, finding in it both refuge and a rest, as her mother had anticipated. But all plans for the future were laid aside or left in the balance till she could know what was to be David's fate.

David was going to get well, the doctors announced one morning, and Julia might go in to see him. But they added a postscript which staggered her in her first wild joy:

"Blind! David blind! Oh, doctor, you mustn't let it be so. Think of his work—his writing," she sobbed.

"I know, I know, my dear," he answered kindly "But we've done more than we at first hoped, to save his life. Poor fellow— someone else will have to be eyes for him now."

"He would rather die, I know he would," she murmured, standing outside the door and dreading to enter. David blind, whose eyes meant life itself with all they were given him to do! How could he wish to live? And she thought with a shudder what it would mean to her if her life-work were suddenly snatched from her and she be left in utter darkness. David blind! She felt a strange embarrassment at the thought of meeting him, as if he were a different person, a stranger.

But when she saw his poor, thin face on the pillow and the bandage about his eyes, she forgot everything in a wave of unutterable pity.

"David!" she cried, her own eyes full of tears, and hurrying across the room she bent over him tenderly.

He groped for her head, breathing quickly. "Julia, poor little girl," he whispered brokenly, smoothing her hair with the lean fingers which were henceforth to be his only eyes. For a few moments they could not speak; she sat beside him holding his hand, which gripped hers hard, as if it was hold upon life itself.

"Well, here I am," he said at last, "a poor, wretched wreck."

"But you're alive, David!" He smiled bitterly.

"Alive! Is it alive to be cooped in darkness which nothing can ever lighten—not even your face, Jule? Oh, to think that I shall never see it again."

He buried his bandaged eyes in his hands and sobbed like a child. She tried to soothe him, but her own lips trembled.

"Think of me, David," she faltered. "It's for me you were saved—for the doctors were working night and day. And I am grateful—oh, so grateful."

"Grateful for a sorry gift, Jule," he said, pressing her hand to his lips.

But here the nurse came in and took her away, saying that the first call must be a short one, for fear of exciting him. And indeed his wan cheek was flushed and his pulse ran high with a fever which she didn't like to see.

The relief of knowing that his life was no longer in actual danger acted like a tonic on Julia's spirits. Her nature was buoyant, and the reaction from that first terrible shock gave her new zest for life. It was a comfort to feel no longer every night her heart growing heavier and heavier with fear as she approached the house, silent and uncommunicative, with its problem of life and death yet unresolved. Though she realized the tragedy of his blindness, it had not yet worn into her soul as a lasting and inescapable evil. Much of her old gaiety returned, and she tried to infuse it into his darkness; but that seemed impossible. He was sunk into a patient melancholy.

One evening he broached the subject which was troubling him. "I've been thinking it all over," he said, "in those dark days while I have lain here. When they thought me unconscious, I was looking with my mind's eye into the future. Everything is changed, Jule. I can make shift to get along upon my little income, but I can't work with you in fair partnership—I should be a drag and a hindrance. You have your own career plain before you. I am not going to keep you back. We will dissolve the partnership, Jule, and I will shut up shop and retire from business."

"Don't talk such nonsense, David," she cried. "You're not going to stop working on account of this mere accident. And as for me— I don't want the partnership dissolved—how can you think it?"

"But I insist that you release me," he went on, trying to assume a cheerful nonchalance which ill accorded with his pathetic face and bandaged eyes. "I know. It's a question of two ruined ambitions or one. My life is spoiled—I don't intend that yours shall be. You needn't say that it would make no difference. I know better. Why, I have listened—you haven't touched the piano these two weeks, all on my account."

She hastened to disclaim the sacrifice, conscious the while that he would have done more for her. "But I've practiced at a neighbor's. You see, it has made no difference."

He was silent a moment. "I'm glad you kept up," he said. "At least then I've done you no injury so far, as I feared. But—your engagement to play next fall? Of course you had the offer?"

She gave a slow assent.

"And you signed with them, I hope?" He knew how her heart had been set upon it.

"I didn't sign till yesterday," she replied reluctantly. "I couldn't promise anything when you were so ill, David. But when I found you were out of danger"—she hesitated—"it was too good a chance to let slip. I sent my acceptance last night."

"That's good!" He spoke brightly, but there was the acceptance of despair in his voice. "What a famous girl you're going to be, Jule! Now tell me all about everything, and would you be so good as to read me the reviews about your concert—the first one—the last one, I—I—the night before. I had my pockets full of them and was coming out here to read them with you—when it happened." His voice broke, but he steadied it again. "There they are, on the table somewhere. Will you read them?"

So she read them all, fulsome flatteries and barefaced compliments, flushing with pride and pleasure which he could not see but felt, and his heart went cold. She stopped suddenly as an involuntary sigh escaped him.

"Oh, David, how selfish I am," she cried. "I'm boring you to death, and you so tired. You must rest now and go to sleep," and she rose to go. But he detained her a moment.

"You must promise me one thing," he said. "I am longing to hear you play again. You won't go out to practice any more, but use your own piano. You will, Julia?"

So she promised.

The days went by slowly and David improved, but was still too weak to be removed to his boarding-place. Julia was very good to him in the intervals of her work. They had no further discussions of the future, and she didn't consider herself disengaged, despite David's words; she would indignantly have denied it to anyone. But the prospect of marriage drew further and further into the indefinite, and instead of a settled date in the summer she thought of it as a vague, remote time when she would devote herself to David's care. But first she must skim the cream of success. At times her heart misgave her and she tried to make up to David for the preoccupation of her hours.

He had given no hint of any desire to commit thought to paper. But she came in one evening with a portfolio, pads of paper, ink, and many pens.

"I have come to be your amanuensis," she announced briskly. "You are not going to give up work like this. I shall keep you at it and write what you tell me, as Milton's daughters did. Now you must think, David."

He shook his head with a sad little smile. "You mustn't neglect your work for mine," he said. "Go back to your piano, Jule." She little knew how often the unsympathetic exercises and tiresome scales brought stinging tears of renunciation to his bandaged eyes. "I haven't anything to write," he said after a pause.

"But you must, David." She was impatient at his seeming indifference to her attentions. *If he knew how tired and cross she was, and how in truth she longed to get to her piano, he would appreciate the sacrifice,* she thought. "You must form the habit of composing just so much every day," she declared. "I shall come in every night and take down what you tell me. So you will accomplish something."

"You are very good," he said patiently. "Perhaps sometimes there will be something. But—I can't plan my work as you do, Jule. I might not think of anything for days; and then again if you were not here when the thought came, I could not perhaps remember. I am afraid I sha'n't do much work any more."

"Nonsense," she retorted. "You can write as well now as ever you could if you have an amanuensis. And here am I to be one. Isn't there anything for me to do, then?"

"There are some business letters to be answered, I think. If you don't mind, the publishers are bothering me for copy, and one thing or another. I should be very grateful."

So she cleared off a part of his accumulated correspondence, and went to rest that night conscious that she had done her duty nobly.

For some days after that she came in every evening prepared to write. But when she found that he never had anything for her to transcribe, it puzzled and annoyed her; and her disappointment troubled and saddened him, as if he felt it his fault rather than his misfortune. He could not tell her how often the fancies went through his brain while she was playing, when he dared not interrupt her. How, when the mood was upon him, he dreaded to call her from her own work. Or how, in the stillness of the night when he lay awake, the only conscious soul in the house, he saw visions with his sightless eyes which day with its sounds—for now it brought only sounds—would soon dispel. There were times when he waited for her eagerly—and she did not come. And at other times when she came there was something in her atmosphere which chilled the glow of enthusiasm and froze the words upon his lips. He had never formerly been conscious of a lack of sympathy. But he had never loved her nor needed her so much before. Then he, too, had been independent and self-poised and ambitious; but never selfish nor forgetful.

After some spasmodic efforts to rouse him to a sense of his duty to art, Julia gave him up in pique. The answering of mere business letters was of no interest to her, and when she found that was all the clerkship he ever required, she ceased to offer her services. Her time was growing too valuable to waste thus. So when she came to see him they merely chatted of her work and prospects, which were growing more important every day. She seemed to be riding on the top wave of success, and chance after chance offered itself for her to become better known and more widely applauded. Hauptmann, her teacher, was delighted with her progress; and from being a stern master was become her devoted slave. She was loaded with compliments and attentions, and her way seemed a path of roses.

David also was progressing—on the road to recovery. But it was no flowery way for him. There came a day when he was well enough to go back to town, Julia and her mother accompanying him as a last attention. She was not sorry to have him go, for his continual presence in the house weighed upon her spirits as a sort of perpetual reproach. In the train they two sat alone together, and this gave opportunity for another long and serious talk, much to the purpose of the former one. But this time Julia was cooler and more willing to be convinced; while he, having gained much in self-control and experience during the past few weeks, was able to be more firm and self-assertive and coldly convincing. He proved to her that her duty was not to him but to herself, her art, and her mother's ambition. He ranged upon his side of the argument her increasing powers and prospects, and spelled her Art with an even larger A than it deserved. He assured her that he was neither help-less nor friendless, and that if he should need an amanuensis, which was not likely, there were plenty to be had. He showed her conclusively that—as she had already taken pains to reassure her-self—she was by no means necessary to his happiness; and he proved that he was more than a stumbling block to her—but the absolute ruin of her ambition. So, after very feeble demurs, she agreed to annul the engagement. Free and unbound! Involuntarily she drew a long breath as they alighted from the car. She did not see the spasm of pain which shot across David's face.

They left him, quite calm and smiling, in the parlor of his boarding-house, where, with a few pleasant words, Mrs. Royce resigned him to the care of his landlady. She meant to be kind, but she was an ambitious woman, and indeed David was manifestly no longer a desirable son-in-law. She knew that he still loved Julia, and was grateful that he had joined with her to bring the girl to reason. It was a great relief to her.

As for David, he stood for a moment facing helplessly the door through which Julia's voice had gone away; then Mrs. Jones led him, stumbling, up the stairs to his little chamber.

It was some weeks later before they saw him again. Mrs. Royce went in with her daughter for a kindly call—she did not intend that the poor fellow should be deserted by his old friends. They found him sadly changed, worn to a shadow of his former self, but with a pale spirituelle beauty which was almost terrible. His eyes were free from the bandages now, and they were as blue as ever; but in their sightless depths was a sadness which cut Julia to the heart. He was very patient and calm when Mrs. Royce asked about his work.

"Mrs. Jones is very kind," he said. "She does whatever little writing I have to attend to now. There are only a few notes to answer, now and then."

"But have you then given up your writing—your composing entirely?" asked Mrs. Royce in surprise. "I had thought you were as devoted to your Muse as—as Julia is to hers. A man with talent like yours should not let *any* obstacle stand in the way."

He flushed through the delicate skin. "There are some obstacles which even devotion cannot surmount," he said quietly. She thought he meant his blindness; but Julia knew better.

"Surely you can find an amanuensis who would give you—who would sell you all his time," she said. "I don't see that one needs eyes in your profession. You see more without them than we do, as it is. But as for me—think how dreadful if anything should happen to my eyes!" the horror in her tone revealing her egoism.

"I hope that will never happen, for the world's sake," he said gently. "As for me—I seem to lack the stimulus to write, as well as the power. It's not my eyes alone which are clouded."

"But your book—the one you were working on when—

before—the unfinished one, I mean." Julia was strangely abashed and uncomfortable.

"It is still unfinished," he said simply. "I think it will always remain so. The publishers have been at me again and again to send them the completed chapters, and I keep putting them off. Maybe I'll feel more like work when my cousin Tom comes. He's very fond of me. He has promised to play scribe for me, for a time at least. You cannot understand—the atmosphere makes such a difference. I could not do anything with an unsympathetic clerk."

"I do hope you'll finish the book," Mrs. Royce said sincerely. "It is sure to be as popular as the others—if you only finish it. I don't know how many people I have heard inquiring for it."

"*If* I finish it," he answered briefly. "It was my favorite. I had put my best into it, I think. Somehow—I haven't anything to piece it out with, now. But we shall see," he made a gesture as of dismissing the whole subject. "I hear you're to play at a very important concert next week," he said brightly, turning toward Julia. "It's a great honor. May you have every success—and fame to your heart's content. You're sure to win wherever you go." His tone was wistful. They rose to depart, each taking his hand kindly. It trembled as Julia's touched it.

"Good morning," she said in a low voice. She was so strangely affected by his words, look, and manner that she hardly dared trust herself to speak. He hesitated a moment before answering, still holding her hand.

"Good-bye," he breathed almost inaudibly. "Good-bye."

David's words rang in her mind constantly on the way home, and she answered her mother's remarks at random or not at all. "I haven't anything left to put into it now"; she was thinking of the pitiful cheerlessness of the boarding-house parlor, wondering how an artistic temperament could endure such an atmosphere. "You can't understand—the atmosphere makes such a difference." She remembered his wistful expression as he said, "Tom is very fond of me," and how her heart had leaped when he turned his sightless eyes toward her. How pale and worn and ill he looked, poor fellow, with no one to encourage or help or take care of him. She bit her lips to keep back the tears which she would not have her mother see.

Julia began to doubt herself. She had an overweening idea of her duty to herself and Art, and she was on the road to fame and success. What could she do? How pause or step aside? And yet, David's voice and David's eyes haunted her. And most of all, that "Good-bye" which he had whispered. What did it mean? Was she going to lose him utterly?—did he have "the foreknowledge of death"?

Every day she went through her work mechanically and without interest. Every night she tossed and turned in sleepless worry; and her pillow was wet with scalding tears. The attentions of Herr Hauptmann grew unbearable. She could not help contrasting him with David, and her heart went sick at her own foolishness.

The concert was another great success—but one of so many that its novelty was gone, and Julia was bored and heartsick of the compliments and flatteries with which she was surfeited. She stood alone and unobserved in a dim corner of the entrance hall, caressing an armful of beautiful roses which had been handed her upon the platform. She was waiting for the carriage which Herr Hauptmann had gone to order for her, glad to escape his odious attentions and fulsome praise. She was thinking even now of David—how pleasant if he were there to do this service for her, and

"It's the Express to New York," she said, "we cannot go back—we don't want to. Come, Mother, and help me find him."

They found him in the second car, wan and worn with the final renunciation and departure.

"David," she whispered softly in his ear, bending over the seat from behind.

He started, flushing crimson. "Her voice," he muttered, "am I dreaming again?" Cousin Tom looked around quickly.

"Miss Royce!" he exclaimed in cold surprise, recognizing the pianiste of the previous evening. Julia went on as if oblivious of his presence, of everything but David's face turned sideways in bewilderment.

"David," she repeated softly, "are you running away from me? I came to bring back your roses, you see." She held one up to his face gently.

"What does it mean?" he stammered. "How did you get here?"

"I couldn't accept flowers that meant good-bye," she said, still more softly.

Tom arose and moved down the car, and Mrs. Royce following him, they sat down together like old friends.

"There isn't going to be any good-bye," Julia went on; "never any more for you and me, David."

He turned white now. "What do you mean?" he asked excitedly. "Don't play with me, Jule. Where are you going?"

"I'm going to New York to be married," she said with playful tenderness, "and so are you, Mr. Colchester. You can't help it, you see, for Mother and I have abducted you, and this is an express train. You can't get off if you want to, David, any more than I can. Do you want to go back, David?" She was sitting on the seat beside him now, and he was holding her hand. But he could not speak.

"It is the old partnership renewed," she went on after a pause full of feeling. "But this time it's for ever and ever, David, till death do us to part. Oh—I'm glad this is an express train, and that we cannot go back."

ABBIE FARWELL BROWN (1881–1927) *was born in Boston, Massachusetts, to a "blue-blooded" family whose American roots date back to the* Mayflower. *After studying at Radcliffe, she went on to author such beloved children's books as* The Lonesomest Doll, The Christmas Angel, The Book of Saints, *and* Friendly Beasts, *and poetry collections such as* A Pocketful of Posies, The Heart of New England, *and* The Silver Stair.

PART III

HEALING

But for you who revere my name, the sun of righteousness
will rise with healing in its wings. And you will go out
and leap like calves released from the stall.

MALACHI 4:2

A MESSAGE
FROM THE SEA

Arthur Gordon

He had been on top of the world. Then came the October 24, 1929, stock market crash—and he had nothing.

He drank himself into a three-day stupor then fled to the ocean, intending to end it all...

At the surf's edge, his bleary eyes were arrested by a shining object in the sand. He stopped.

———

Some people in this world have a marvelous gift—have you noticed this? When you're in trouble, or have some aching problem, you turn to them instinctively. Something in them draws you like a magnet. It's hard to say exactly what this quality is: a kind of serenity, an inner strength, a generosity of spirit.

Whatever it is, I have a friend who has this quality for me. So the other night, when something was weighing on my mind, I called him up.

"Sure," he said. "Come on over. Alma's gone to bed and I'm lost in the wastelands of television. I'll heat up the coffee."

So I went over, and at the end of an hour—just as I knew I would—I felt a lot better. The problem was still there, but it didn't seem so frightening, somehow. Not with Ken sitting in his old swivel chair, feet up on the desk, hands locked behind his head, not saying much, just listening and…and *caring*.

Suddenly the gratitude and affection I felt seemed to need expression. "Ken," I said, "when it comes to smoothing out wrinkles in troubled minds, you're wonderful. How do you do it?"

He has a slow smile that seems to start in his eyes. "Well," he said, "I'm a good deal older than you."

I shook my head. "Age has nothing to do with it. There's a calmness in you that goes very deep. Where does it come from? Where did you get it?"

He didn't say anything for a few seconds. He just looked at me pensively, as if trying to make up his mind whether to tell me something or not. Finally, with the toe of his shoes, he pulled open one of the desk drawers. From it he took a small, oblong box made of cardboard. He put it on the blotter.

"If I do have any of this quality you're talking about," he said, "it probably comes from this."

I waited. On the mantel behind me, a clock ticked.

Ken picked up one of his blackened pipes and began to load it. "You've only known me for—how long? Ten years? Twelve? This box is a lot older than that. I've had it more than thirty years. Alma's the only other person who knows what's in it, and maybe she's forgotten by now. But I take it out and look at it now and then…"

A match flared; the smoke curled, blue and reflective, in the lamplight. "Back in the twenties," Ken said in a faraway voice, "I

was a successful young man in Manhattan. I made money fast and spent it faster. I was the golden boy, able to out-drink or out-think anybody. I married Alma because she was pretty and decorative, but I don't think I loved her. I don't think there was any love in me, really. The closest thing to it was the very high regard that I had— for myself."

I stared at him in amazement. I found it almost impossible to believe this brutal self-portrait.

"Well," said Ken, "as you've probably anticipated, the day of reckoning came. And it was quite a day. It's hard for people who didn't go through the Wall Street crash to know what it was like. One week I was a millionaire—on paper, anyway. The next I was a pauper. My reaction was predictable: I got drunk and stayed drunk for three days."

He gave a short bark of a laugh and stood up, running one hand through his wiry hair. "The place I chose for this little orgy of self-pity was a beach cottage that we owned—or rather, *had* owned before the bottom fell out of our gilded cage. Alma wanted to come with me, but I wouldn't let her. I just wanted to get away from everything and drink myself blind, and that's just what I did.

"But the time comes when you begin to sober up. For an alcoholic—and I was close to being one—this can be a ghastly experience. You're overwhelmed with self-disgust; you're choked with despair. I looked at my face in the mirror; the bloodshot eyes, the three-day beard, and knew I was looking at a total failure. As a man, as a husband, as a human being, it seemed to me that I had made a complete mess of my life. The thought came to me that the best thing I could do for Alma and everyone would be to remove myself from the scene—permanently.

"I knew, moreover, just how to do it. A half-gale was blowing outside; the sea was wild. I would swim out as far as I could, past the point of no return. That would take care of everything."

Ken's pipe had gone out; he put it on the desk. The old chair creaked as he sat down. "When you're driven to a decision like that, your one thought is to get it over with. So I wasted no time. I stumbled down the porch steps—still half-drunk, I guess—and onto the beach. It was just after dawn, I remember; the sky was red and angry; the waves were furious. I walked straight down to the edge of the water. As I reached it, something glinted on the sand."

He opened the box. "This."

In the box was a shell. Not a particularly unusual shell; I had seen others like it. A narrow oval of fluted calcium; pale, graceful, delicate.

"I stood there staring at it," Ken went on. "Finally I picked it up, wet and glistening. It was so fragile that the least pressure of my fingers would have crushed it. Yet here it was, undamaged, perfect.

"How was this possible? The question seemed to seize upon my mind, while all around me the wind shrieked and the ocean roared. Tons of seething water had flung this shell on the hard-packed sand. It should have been smashed to splinters, utterly destroyed. But it wasn't.

"What had kept the shell intact, unbroken? I kept asking myself with a kind of frantic urgency, and suddenly I knew. Or thought I knew. There had been no panic in the shell—no pride, no bitterness, no struggle, no despair. It had yielded itself to the awful forces crashing around it. It had accepted the storm just as it had accepted the stillness of the depths where it had its beginnings. By not resisting, it had survived. And suddenly I saw myself—battling against the inevitable, beating my fists against fate—when I should have been accepting whatever life sent, accepting with faith, enduring with faith.

"I don't know how long I stood there, but finally, when I turned away from the sea, I took the shell with me. I've had it ever since."

I took the box from my friend and lifted out the shell. It lay in my hand, untouched by the years, exquisitely wrought, feather-light. "Do you know its name?" I asked him.

Ken smiled that slow smile of his. "Yes," he said, "I know. They call it an Angel's Wing."

ARTHUR GORDON (1912–) *still lives and writes from his natal seacoast near Savannah, Georgia. During his long and memorable career, he edited such renowned magazines as* Good Housekeeping, Cosmopolitan, *and* Guideposts. *He is the author of a number of books, including* Reprisal *(1950),* Norman Vincent Peale: Minister to Millions *(1958),* A Touch of Wonder *(1983), and* Return to Wonder *(1996), as well as several hundred short stories.*

THE MAKING OF MIKE

Irving Bacheller

Each of us faces troubles, large and small, but not many of us could even imagine facing what Mike did. Even fewer of us could imagine *doing* what he did.

———

Mike (Michael) Dowling was born in Huntington, Massachusetts, in 1866. As a boy, he was profoundly disinterested in books. He knew which was the prettiest girl in school, and which boy had the best jackknife, and such items of information, but he rarely knew his lessons. At ten, he could read, write, and cipher, and while his knowledge embraced other things—such as the shape of the earth and the names of the presidents—these latter items were, he thought, largely decorative and unnecessary. He never ran away from school, but he had a truant mind. It generally rode a pony and indulged in the pleasure of roping steers and shooting Indians. He wanted to be a cowboy. He had read all about the life out on the Western plains, in a newspaper.

Mike's mother died when he was ten. That set him free. He

went west with the definite purpose of becoming a rich cattleman. He was big and strong for his age.

When he was fourteen, he got a job as cattle herder in Yellow Medicine County, Minnesota. They gave him a good pony and a herd of five hundred cattle. He knew a lot about cattle and the arts of the cowboy. He bought a big revolver on credit at the herder's store, and went to his task. At first he thought it was great fun. The prairies lay flat and green till they seemed to touch the rounded dome of the sky. For a week or two they interested him. But he was all alone with his herd on that vast floor of the heavens. It was like a great silent room. He felt very small and lonely, but the cattle would have nothing to do with him. They seemed to distrust his character and demand references. Winds hurried by, hissing in the tall grass, and birds rode upon them.

These were his only companions—these and the cattle—save when he went to the store for supplies, and then he was always in a hurry.

Now cattle—even five hundred cattle—and a big revolver are poor company for a human being. Mike grew weary of them. He did brave deeds. His devotion to duty had been quite heroic one day when the herd took to flight in a storm, but there had been nobody to see and applaud him. He was homesick, but too faithful to desert his task. The whistles of locomotives came faintly to his ear now and then from far away, and seemed to be calling him. The herd drifted back and forth through a range some ten miles in diameter, and there were three rude shacks in which he lived.

It was probably good for Mike. It gave him an excellent chance to enlarge his acquaintance with himself. He began to explore his own mind. It seemed to be about as empty as the sky. He found there the list of the presidents and the multiplication table, and not much more. He tried to interest himself by looking them over. He

reminded himself of the proportions of land and water and the shape of the world, but as an entertainer Mike decided that he was no good. If he had only known the Declaration of Independence it would have been a great comfort to him. He saw that he didn't know enough to be good company. October came, and cold winds out of the north, and time dragged as the end of his solitary confinement drew near. He got rid of the herd on the fourth of December.

Canby was the business center for the farmers whose stock he had herded. There he received his pay. Two farmers had driven to the little village that afternoon in a lumber wagon. Mike was to ride with them to a farm where he had left his pony, six miles away. He held their team in the cold wind for a number of hours while the two men were drinking inside. He and the horses were chilled to the bone. But men don't worry about boys and horses when they're having a good time. Finally, when dusk began to fall, the horses began to rear and plunge. Mike shouted for help. The men buttoned their overcoats, hurried out, quieted the horses, and took the spring seat in the wagon.

Then the winter of the great snows arrived—the winter of 1880. The old settlers have never ceased to talk about it. The storms came like a resistless army, spreading their white tents on the roofs of other tents, until Minnesota was buried to the tops of its telegraph poles.

A lumber wagon with its party was going out to meet the first battalion in this great army. It hurried, but the sky was black and the wind struck hard. Soon a gale was blowing. It seemed to be trying to push them back. It whistled in the leather of the harness and the timbers of the wagon. The men on the front seat quickly turned their heads when the first missiles of icy snow struck them.

Leaves and wisps of grass were flying in the wind. There were strange noises before and above them.

The dusk had thickened. They didn't see the great, white, rushing, swirling, diluted avalanche until it fell upon them. It checked team and wagon with a jolt, for the air had suddenly thickened. It was as if the very heavens were falling. Away northward great banks of wet air, a league deep at least and belike a thousand miles wide, had frozen suddenly. Their moisture had gone hurtling toward the earth. It struck the current of an arctic hurricane. This hardened the soft snow and whipped and churned it into pinpoints of ice. These were massed thickly by the pressure of the blast. There were probably thousands of them in a cubic inch of the air. The men on the front seat covered their faces with mittened hands. One shouted to the other, but was unheard. They could see only the tails of the horses. The driver gave up trying to steer them. In the back, sitting on a shoebox, was Mike, head bowed and ears begging for shelter. His hands were so cold that he could no longer feel the box to which he clung. He felt a sense of being smothered by the stinging sky dust.

The wagon began to jump. The horses had lost the road and were crossing a plowed field. Suddenly they quickened their pace. A big jolt broke the hold of Mike's numb hands and pitched him out of the wagon. He picked himself up and shouted, his voice sounding to his own ears like that of a man calling from a distance. The wagon had gone out of sight, but he could faintly hear the rattle of its wheels. He ran toward it, eager as a sprinter in a race. That little straw of sound was his only hope of safety. When he stopped to get his breath he could no longer hear it. The storm had so darkened the sky that he couldn't even see the wheel tracks, not even if he were near them. Then Mike knew that somewhere in the darkness of that night his life was likely to end. He had heard that a man lost in a Minnesota blizzard had as good a chance of living as at the bottom of the sea.

Mike was chilled to the bone. The ice dust in the fling of a seventy-mile wind had scoured his eyes and rubbed the skin off one side of his face. He could hear it strike his cheeks and forehead. Feathers of ice kept forming over his eyes. But Mike didn't give up. He knew that he must keep moving, or his blood would turn to ice, like water in a frozen pipe. So he pulled down his cap, turned the side of his head to the wind, and hurried on. Slowly the push of the storm faced him about until he was going with it. Often he had to stop to get his breath. The effort of breathing seared his nose, and it was hard work to get enough of the speeding, snow-filled air to fill his lungs.

Hour after hour he labored in the noisy, flying dungeon of the blizzard, seeing nothing. Now and then he would brush the ice and snow from his eyes and then imagine for a moment that he saw lights ahead. It was when he was wading in a drift that he decided to lie down and rest for just a minute. The strangest of all emotions, self-fear, came on him. He trembled and ran a few steps, as if he hoped thereby to get away from it. He grew angry. He called himself a vile name, but the thought of rest kept stealing back upon him. Often it begged and pleaded for a moment's stop, but Mike drove it away as one would drive a thieving dog from a pantry. Suddenly he looked ahead and lo! the sun was shining on green fields, and it was a still summer day, and there was his home, with his mother and father on the doorstep. They saw him coming and were waving their hands. What a long sleep he would have in that little bedroom upstairs! Then the icy darkness once more roared across the prairie.

His breast bumped against something in his path and woke

him. He was still traveling in the storm. What was it that his mittens touched? It gave as he touched it. He felt it over carefully. It was stove wood, corded breast high. There must be a house, but where? Ten feet would be as bad as a mile if he went wrong. How could he find the house? He called again and again, but got no answer. He climbed to the top of the stack and picked up a stick of wood and threw it into the darkness as far as he could, hoping to hit one of the buildings.

The stick fell silently. He threw the wood in all directions, but it seemed only to hit the air. He gave up, got off the stack, and went on. In a moment he ran into a heap of straw. He couldn't resist its invitation. He began to burrow into it. He was like a fox driven to its hole with baying hounds close behind him. He flung the loose straw aside and burrowed fiercely with his hands, and crept headfirst deep into the straw pile and rolled on his back.

His will to sleep came strong and cunning as a wolf in sight of its prey. Desperately he fought against it. The enemy would overcome and drag him into slumber, and then he would drive it away. For hours this lonely struggle of life against death continued.

By and by he began to creep out of the straw. Thank God, he could see light! What? Yes. The sun was shining. The storm had passed. Deep snow glistened in the light. There was the house not a hundred feet from where he lay, and smoke was coming out of its chimney. The smoke had a friendly look. No, he was not dreaming now. It was real sunlight, real smoke! He got to his feet and fell sidewise. His legs felt like a pair of stilts. He rose and fell again. He couldn't stand. He began to creep toward the house on his hands and knees. Something had hurt a little. He stopped and looked. It was one of the sticks of wood that he had thrown into the darkness. He tried to pick it up and toss it aside, but his hands wouldn't obey him. His thumb and fingers refused to work. He got to the door and struck it with the back of his hand. The sound was like that of a stone striking the timber. He looked at his hand. It was as stiff as if it had been stuck full of needles. He heard footsteps and voices, and then the door opened. He felt the warm air of the room and saw a man standing in the doorway.

"What's the matter?" asked the man.

"Been out all night in the storm," said Mike as he knelt on the doorstep.

The man leaned over and looked into his face.

"Don't you know you're froze, boy?"

"I know it. I'm just a chunk of ice," said Mike.

The man and his wife lifted the boy to his feet, helped him through the doorway, and set him down.

Then they ran from the room like a pair of scared rabbits. One brought a wash boiler full of snow, the other a pail of water from the well. The woman poured the water on the snow while the man tried to remove Mike's boots. "He's shot full of frost, and the leather is nailed to his legs!" said he. "We'll have to cut 'em off."

He slit the boots and stockings from top to toe with his knife and stripped them off, and put Mike's legs in the icy water. Meanwhile the woman had pulled off his mittens and immersed his hands. Then she began to rub his face and ears with the wet snow. Mike writhed and groaned as the frost coming out formed a sheath of ice on his feet, legs, and hands. It was like pulling needles. Then nature had its struggle in trying to reconnect its countless nerves and channels so long clogged and cut off. The boy bore it bravely, and all that day the man and woman worked on him. They succeeded in drawing the frost, but his hands and feet were swollen and powerless. The blizzard had begun again, and they couldn't go for the doctor, who lived nine miles away. So they put Mike to bed. It was all they could do for him.

Three days passed before they could get the doctor—days of great agony for poor Mike. The doctor declared that he was beyond help. His hands and the lower ends of his legs were already dead. There was a chance an operation would save the rest of him, depending on his vitality. The doctor had brought his instruments and all the ether and chloroform he'd been able to buy in the little town where he practiced. He didn't have enough, however, for the big job ahead of him. It was hard on Mike, and it exhausted the doctor and the man and woman who helped him. The boy went through it bravely and clung to his life and passed the danger point. Strength was slow in returning to him.

"So what to do now?" they asked him.

Since his father was poor, Mike would not permit himself to be thrown upon him. He insisted that the State should take care of him. He *insisted*. Both feet and one hand were gone, but the doctor had saved the thumb and the main part of his left hand. He could get about somewhat in the fashion of a monkey. The charity commissioner arranged for his keep at a farmhouse.

Now the whips of pain and loss and pride had had a remarkable effect on the boy. His brain was awake at last. His spirit began to feel its strength. He devised a plan and then a proposition to the commissioner. If the State would give him a set of artificial limbs and a year in school, he would release it from all further liability. The proposition to the commissioner was accepted. They took him to Chicago, where he was fitted with new feet and a right hand. Soon he was able to walk as upright and as steadily as ever.

His schooling began. With his one thumb he could hold a pen or a pencil and turn the pages of his books. Mike had been stripped pretty bare: he had but his brain and one year in which to make it a useful possession. He sat one night thinking of these two assets. He took his pencil and began to make figures. His brain was as good as ever; and he now calculated that the year had only three hundred and sixty-five days, but there would be more than a million minutes in it. Most boys of his age would need at least five years for an education—that meant, say, two and a half million minutes. There were fourteen hundred and forty minutes in a day. He figured out how boys generally spent their time. It was about as follows:

> 540 minutes in bed
> 180 minutes in eating, bathing, dressing, and undressing
> 180 minutes in play
> 120 minutes in sheer idleness
> 210 minutes in school dalliance
> 210 minutes in study

Mike decided to spend:

> 420 minutes in bed
> 50 minutes in eating, bathing, dressing, and undressing
> <u>940</u> minutes in study in and out of school
> 1,410 minutes total

This schedule would enable him to put five years of the average boy's effort into the one year ahead of him. Thereafter that year became, in his view, a collection of minutes. Of course he would need exercise, but he could be going over his lessons while he walked to and from school and did chores.

The teacher, seeing the boy's eagerness to learn, spent many evenings helping him in his arithmetic and algebra. Mike strode ahead of his classes. He was the wonder and the talk of the neighborhood. He began to enjoy one by-product of which he had never thought—the fruit of good advertising. The intensive method of study that he had adopted had advertised him as a unit of power in the community. But Mike didn't pose as a born phenomenon. He merely credited it all to hard work.

At the end of the year the value of that advertising began to show itself, and he got a license to teach. He taught seven years, the last three as head of the Renville High School.

He was elected to the lower house of the State legislature in 1900, and served for two sessions as its speaker. In his political work he won the friendship of President William McKinley, who sent him to the Philippines as a special commissioner.

Soon after his work began there he went to see the sultan of Sulu to engage his interest in the cause of education. The sultan was bored and refused to listen. Something had to be done to catch the attention of the barbarian monarch. Mike first removed his right hand and threw it on the floor between them. In half a moment he had taken off both his feet and tossed them before the astonished sultan. He caught his head between his elbow and left hand and began to turn it as if intending to add that to the pile. The sultan ran to his side with a look of delight, saying:

"Keep your head on. I want to talk with you and learn the secret of your magic."

Mike held up his one thumb and told his story to the sultan, who learned what a man may accomplish in America with one thumb and a brain and the will to make the most of them.

IRVING BACHELLER (1859–1950) *was born in Pierpoint, New York. Although he wrote a number of short stories, he is best known for novels such as* Eben Holden, Silas Strong, A Man for the Ages, *and* In the Days of Poor Richard. *He reached his peak of productivity during the first third of the twentieth century.*

The Wall of Silence

Shirley Barksdale

Ronnie was dead...and no one, it seemed, would ever talk about him again. In that regard, he was twice dead.

It took his saucy daughter, a number of years later, to bring his memory back.

Our son died at age twenty-four, leaving his young wife and an infant daughter. After the first hard edge of grief softened and I could once more speak his name, I discovered that to do so created an air of awkwardness among friends and relatives. They clammed up, averted their eyes, or quickly changed the subject. Those few people who spoke of him did so with such tones of gloom that they perpetuated our sorrow.

In time, I learned to drop my son's name from my conversation and to let his memory lie quietly in my heart.

Although my husband continued to attend church, I gradually ceased to go. I simply could not trust my emotions when I heard the familiar hymns our son so often had sung. Nor could I control the slow, relentless anger, like an insidious disease, that gnawed away at my faith. *Where was God,* I wondered, *on that night when our son's car skidded on an icy street and plunged him to his death?*

Eventually his widow remarried, and her husband legally adopted our grandchild. We rejoiced in their happiness, but the adoption process once more erased the name of our son. His daughter had a brand-new identity.

Soon afterward, my husband and I were transferred to California. At first, I welcomed the change promised by the move; I thought leaving behind Colorado and all its memories to embrace a new lifestyle would hasten the healing.

Instead, I missed my friends and, mostly, I missed watching our granddaughter grow up. By the time we moved back to Denver years later, she had been transformed from a feisty toddler into a charming teenager.

Upon our return, our granddaughter, her mother, and her stepfather welcomed us warmly, but those years apart left my husband and me feeling as if we were guests instead of family.

That first December back in Colorado, while addressing holiday cards, I came to the name of a long-time friend, Diane. I hesitated. Her husband had died a few months earlier, and it seemed inappropriate to send her the stereotypical greeting of "Merry Christmas and a Happy New Year."

This would be her first Christmas without Ken. Remembering the pain of those "firsts," I decided against the usual cheery holiday greeting. Instead, within the folds of a special friendship card I slipped a note, telling her how much we missed Ken, his warmth, his humor and, above all, his remarkable faith that a kidney transplant would come in time. It didn't, but he accepted God's will and harbored no bitterness. How I wish I'd had his spiritual and emotional strength.

The instant I dropped the card into the mailbox, I suffered

tremendous anxiety. *Had I overstepped my role, stirred up painful memories?* I worried. *Was Diane one of those survivors who prefer not to discuss the deceased?*

A few days later, Diane called to acknowledge my note, her voice damp with tears.

"Oh, Di," I wailed. "I'm so sorry. I didn't want to make you cry."

"No, no," she quickly reassured me. "I'm crying out of sheer relief. You're the first person to mention Ken's name so freely. It's so important to know that he's not forgotten."

My own wall of silence regarding my son began to crumble when my granddaughter, still in her teens, came to me and said, "Nana, I never got to know my dad, and now I want to hear all about him."

Surprised and thrilled, I began slowly, speaking his name aloud, "Ronnie." I cherished the sound of it as together we explored his brief life.

My granddaughter reveled in hearing of her father's triumphs and losses and his musical talent, which she clearly had inherited. Before she left that day she asked, "Do you think we could make a memory book of my dad?"

Thus began many happy hours of discovery for her, bittersweet nostalgia for me. We compiled photos of him from infancy to marriage, including a shot of Ronnie holding his daughter just minutes after her birth.

As we sifted through the boxes of memorabilia, we came across a yellowed church program with Ronnie listed as the soloist on Youth Day.

"I wish you could have heard him," I said. "He sang 'Amazing Grace' just the way I like it: sort of jazzed up, with a touch of the blues."

She gave me an impish grin, and in it I saw the reflection of her father.

"Nana, next week I'm going to sing my first solo. Will you and Gramps come to church to hear me?"

How could we refuse? On that windy, sunless day, the church seemed cold, unwelcoming. I sat there, chilled, uncomfortable in my diminished faith and conscious of my conflict with God, wishing fervently that I had not come.

Then our granddaughter stepped forward and sang "Just a Closer Walk with Thee" loud and clear, a bit jazzy, then softly. Just the way I like it.

When the final notes faded, the sun, as if on cue, broke through the overcast sky and turned the stained-glass windows into a warm, rosy glow. In that moment my clenched fists relaxed, the knot of anger in my heart melted, and I knew that God had worked through my granddaughter to reach me.

SHIRLEY BARKSDALE *is a freelance writer who lives and writes from Highlands Ranch, Colorado.*

THE RAGGED CLOAK

Margaret E. Sangster Jr.

Darius was an outcast, for no one wanted anything to do with a hunchback.

But here was this lovely lady whose "time had come," and she smiled at him. When had anyone ever smiled at him?

Darius was tired, desperately tired, and yet he wasn't nearly finished with the day's work. Even though the twilight had come he wasn't finished. There were mangers still to be filled with hay, faintly sweet from last year's clover. There was an earthen floor still to be swept so that the animals, as tired as he, could rest in cleanliness during the night. Darius wished futilely that he were an animal.

If he were an animal, somebody would be filling a manger for him, somebody would be brushing the stable floor for his comfort. And furthermore, if he were an animal, he wouldn't be lonely, for the animals thought only of eating and sleeping and huddling together for protection. As long as Darius could recall he had never known anyone who had worried about his welfare. His food had been scraps from the inn kitchen. His sleeping had been done in a corner which the animals left vacant, and when he felt the need of protection there was no one to lean against.

Stooping low, Darius lifted a great armful of fragrant hay. The stooping hurt him—not more than it always did, not less—for when a boy wears a hump between his shoulders the slightest movement can cause exquisite agony. Darius had never been without that agony—insofar as he knew—the hump had been between his shoulders since his birth. They had told him at the inn that some caravan must have abandoned him near their gate when he was scarcely able to crawl, and they, in pity, had given him refuge. They had told him, also, that their kindness, which had saved his life, must be paid for—a whole lifetime of work would scarcely make up for it. Darius had accepted the verdict—it was a verdict—as he had accepted everything else, stoically.

When he had been just able to stagger about, hardly big enough to run errands, they had thought of training him to be a servant in the inn itself where the quarters were more pleasant and where there were human beings, not animals, for company. But once a guest—a fine lady, sipping wine—had screamed shrilly at the sight of him and had said, "A hunchback! He nauseates me!" And once a man had accused the innkeeper of housing monsters. So Darius had been sent to the stable where people wouldn't be troubled by the sight of him.

Darius, sighing, laid his fragrant burden in a manger and went to the haystack for another armload. A lamb, so small that it was still wobbly on its knock-kneed legs, bumped against him, and Darius stroked the soft head with a work-roughened hand. A cow mooed gently, and a donkey, in from a day of hauling heavy loads, stretched its neck and brayed. Darius thought almost bitterly that animals accepted him as one of themselves, even though people did not.

He thrust a carrot into the tired donkey's mouth and patted the nose of the gentle cow. Animals, he told himself, did not see his distorted frame. They did not avert their gaze from him. They looked to him for the necessities that made it possible for them to exist. To them he was a superior being. Even though he walked haltingly, he walked on two legs instead of four.

Suddenly there was a commotion in the inn courtyard. Darius wondered if there were more guests asking for shelter and reflected that, if such were the case, they would be out of luck.

The inn was filled to overflowing. Throngs were coming to Bethlehem to pay the new taxes which were on everybody's tongue and conscience.

He went to the door of the stable and swung it open, gathering his ragged cloak about his shoulders because the air was bitterly cold outside. There was a man standing in the courtyard. He was holding a donkey—more weary than the little donkey that had brayed—by its bridle. And on the donkey's back, drooping and yet oddly tense, was a woman. As Darius stood in the doorway, listening, he heard the man's voice raised in argument with the innkeeper.

"You *must* take her in," he heard the man say. "She can't travel a step farther. Her time has come."

Darius, his pitying glance on the woman who was swaying perilously in her saddle, wondered what it meant—"her time has come." Was the woman dying? He shuddered with premonition as the innkeeper's voice said curtly, "There is no room in the inn, I tell you. I'm sorry, but there's no room."

The man answered, "but she must lie down immediately. Surely you can see—" His voice broke and he addressed the woman who swayed in the saddle. "Mary," he said, "the pain—can you bear it?"

"Yes, I can bear pain," said a woman's voice, and Darius, who also had learned to bear the weight of suffering, felt a prickling sensation in his twisted spine. Never had he heard a voice so low, so sweet, so tragic. He made a short, jerking step forward and called, "The stable is warm and clean."

The innkeeper turned swiftly. The man who was holding the donkey's bridle gave a little exclamation of relief, and the woman on the donkey's back raised her head. Across the purple twilight of the inn courtyard her eyes sought the eyes of Darius, the hunch-back, and then suddenly she smiled, and her smile had the unearthly tragic sweetness of her voice. "I can indeed lie in the stable," she said. "The lad is kind. Joseph, carry me into the stable."

Scrambling hastily back from the doorway, Darius—his own agony somehow forgotten—found that he was spasmodically gath-ering up great armfuls of hay and throwing them into a corner—the corner farthest removed from the animals. He wanted to do something for this woman who had smiled at him, ignoring his grotesque body. He wanted to do something to make her smile again.

The hay would not be as soft as an inn bed, of course, but it was blessed by the memories of sunshine and flowers growing wild. Only, the thought struck him, hay was prickly. Would a woman who was weary and ill rest in comfort on it, or would the sharp spikes torture her delicate skin? Swiftly he jerked the shabby cloak from his shoulders, and laid it across the golden hay. The innkeeper came striding through the doorway, and the man, walking care-fully, with the woman in his arms, was following behind. The don-key made up the end of the procession.

Darius, cold without his cloak, felt a sense of surging tender-ness that blotted out the chill. He stood aside as the man named Joseph laid the woman on the improvised bed. When the tiny lamb came blundering forward he pushed it aside, but very gently. The innkeeper, glancing at him, said, "Can you keep the animals out of the way, Darius, while—" He nodded mutely, and the innkeeper muttered, "I'll try to send one of the serving girls to help out, if possible. But we're overcrowded with guests, and I'm not sure I can spare anybody,"

He hurried away as if he were glad to be rid of a responsibility for which he had not bargained, and the man, Joseph, fell on his knees beside the woman and touched her hand almost shyly with one of his huge fingers. "The pain?" he asked, "is it getting worse, Mary?"

The woman said, as she had said before, "I can bear it," and the man turned to Darius. "Boy," he said, "bring a lantern and water. Hot water if you can get it."

Darius, child of the stable, living with animals for almost as long as he could remember, brought the lantern and went limping off to the inn kitchen for hot water. When he returned with a basin the woman was lying, apparently composed, on the straw. Her face was calm, but the hands at her sides were clenched into tight knots of torture. As Darius set the basin beside her she turned her head ever so slightly and the smile flashed at him again.

In that stable animals had been born—ewes and goats and calves and even a tiny colt. Darius had sensed, time and again, the struggle and the shadow of death and the ultimate victory. But though the shadow of death was close, this woman named Mary did not struggle, and when the final victory came it was as much a victory of the spirit as of the flesh.

During the hours between dusk and midnight Darius forgot that he was a hunchback, forgot that he was cold, forgot everything save his concern for another sufferer. He kept in the background with the animals. He fetched Joseph the hot water he required, at regular intervals. He fed the little donkey that had brought the woman to this meeting place with destiny. And when the Baby finally lay in its mother's arms, he felt a kinship with Him that he had never felt with anything in his life.

The Baby didn't look newborn. He looked as if the world He had just entered had always been His home. His eyes, widely blue, were eyes that might have gazed across vast distances.

It was Joseph who lifted the Baby away from the mother and laid Him in a manger, but it was Darius who brought Mary a cup of new milk and who supported her as she drank it. It was Joseph who shaded the light of the lantern and composed the woman on her bed of straw, but it was Darius's cloak that kept the straw from scratching her.

Darius, who had never known the accepted words of a prayer, was close to praying without words as he made his way across the stable floor and opened the door just a crack to let in air that, though biting, was fresh. It was only when he peered through the slit-like opening that he realized how bright the courtyard was. He thought at first that the inn was burning, so brilliantly were trees and buildings etched against the night. And then he saw that the radiance came from the sky, for directly over the stable a great star hung in the heavens—a star so white and wonderful that it almost frightened Darius. Yet it didn't really frighten him, for something in the starshine made him think of the woman's smile.

Other people were aware of the starlight, too. The inn servants were rushing to an open space so that they might gaze upward. The innkeeper and his wife were with their servants.

"It's an omen," someone shouted, and then Darius was conscious of a small procession of men coming down the road in the distance. He thought at first that they were robbers. But when they came near, he saw from their shabby coats and the crooks they carried that they were shepherds.

Shepherds from the hills! As they entered the inn courtyard Darius was conscious of the words they were saying. "The angels have spoken to us," one man exulted. "A Savior has been born," another one shouted, "and He is lying in a manger." A third shrilled, "Take us to the Savior that we may worship Him."

They came crowding into the stable, brushing past Darius in

their haste. After the shepherds came the inn servants and the innkeeper and his wife. Darius, shrinking back against the door frame, saw that the Baby in the manger was awake and that His tiny hands were lifted as if in a benediction. He saw that the woman who had given birth to the Baby was raising herself from the bed of straw that he had prepared, that her smile was more radiant than ever.

Before the wonder and pathos of that scene the shepherds fell on their knees and their rough faces reflected a glory that they could scarcely comprehend. The servants dropped, also, to their knees, and the innkeeper muttered under his breath, "Perhaps I could have made room in the inn had I known." It was the innkeeper's wife, starting forward, who quietly removed the ragged cloak upon which Mary had been resting and laid her own linen apron in its place.

Darius, standing by the doorway, followed the cloak with his eyes. He saw it drop, useless and empty, to the stable floor. And all at once, with his whole soul ablaze, he wanted to touch it and have it touch him. It was no longer just a piece of threadbare cloth that had sheltered him from the cold—it was part of the woman, and a part of the Baby who was flesh of her flesh, and a part of the starlight that was making the whole courtyard bright, and part of the message that the angels had brought to shepherds on a hillside. Quietly he crossed the stable floor to where the cloak was lying. Quietly and proudly he lifted it from the floor and wrapped it around his aching shoulders. And as the shepherds, kneeling, whispered, "Glory to God in the highest!" Darius, staring across their bent heads, saw that the woman was watching him and that the Baby in the manger, His head turned ever so slightly, seemed to be watching too.

And then, as he stood clutching the cloak about his shoulders,

Darius felt agony going out of him, felt confidence and strength flowing into him. And as the cloak clung to his back he felt the hump between his shoulders melt away, and he felt his body straighten until it was as tall and firm and gallant as a young tree.

All at once he, too, was kneeling, and though he said brokenly with the others, "Glory to God in the highest!" he was unaware of his own voice speaking. He was conscious only of the woman's smile and of the Baby's tiny upraised fingers.

MARGARET E. SANGSTER JR. (1894–1981) *was born in Brooklyn, New York. An editor, scriptwriter, journalist, short-story writer, and novelist, she was one of the best known and most beloved inspirational writers of the early part of the twentieth century.*

THE FIRING
OF DONALD CAPEN

Alice Louise Lee

Donald Capen had been trained by his parents to always do and say the honest thing. But he found in the big city that believing in such principles was far different from having to *live* them. Being fired was only the beginning, and things only got worse from then on. He began to wonder, *Am I being a fool?*

The youngest clerk in the shipping-house of the Bohr Brothers sat, heavy-hearted, at his desk—the fifth—one Monday morning in June. In front of him an open window admitted the breezes from Lake Erie, while the docks, many stories below, sent up a confusion of sounds from loaded drays and shouting drivers.

These louder noises Donald scarcely heard, so alive was he to the creak of the outer door as it admitted the many clerks and stenographers in the employ of the Bohr Brothers. Finally it opened wide with a rush, and closed with a bang which announced the arrival of the senior member of the firm, Robert Bohr. Donald drew in his breath sharply. He had hoped that Richard Bohr would be in the office that morning.

The elder Bohr strode through the long room, looking neither to the right nor the left. He was a tall man, thin, blond, and irascible in temper.

"If you suit here," Greeley had informed Donald on his second day, "the old man will seem to ignore you, but, nevertheless, you'll get a speedy rise in salary. If you don't suit him, your head will come off with the hair singed! If once you disobey orders you'll find out what I mean."

Donald had disobeyed orders.

Shortly after the swinging door of the private office had ceased its agitated motions, the head clerk, without a glance toward the fifth desk, tapped on the glass of the door and disappeared within. "I shall report you in the morning!" the head clerk had exclaimed, angrily, to Donald twenty-four hours earlier.

Donald glanced up and nodded with assumed cheerfulness. Then his pen moved on, but not as steadily as usual. It was responding to the excited throbs of his pulses.

Greeley came across the room to get in a last word before it should be too late. Greeley had been in the employ of the Bohr Brothers a year, and had been ignored by Robert Bohr without having his salary raised or his hair singed. He was inclined to patronize the quiet newcomer, and had introduced him to his own little social circle.

"Now see here, Capen," Greeley reasoned, bending over Donald's shoulder, "you'd better knuckle under. That thing doesn't hap-

pen right along, you know; and, after all, you're no better than the rest of us."

"I'm not measuring you or any one else by my standard, Greeley!" exclaimed Donald.

The voice of the head clerk sounded from the swinging door: "Mr. Capen, you are wanted in the office."

Five minutes later Donald stood beside the table in the private office, holding in his hand a check, which represented his salary to date. His face was white, and his lips were pressed closely together. Being of Scotch descent, he found silence more golden than speech when facing such a vocal tornado as the senior partner had just expended on him.

The storm had spent itself without producing its usual effect. Donald had not "knuckled under." This unexpected result caused a curious change in the senior Bohr. The angry flush faded from his cheeks, and his eyes, resuming their steel-gray sharpness, searched the young man's face shrewdly. He hesitated a moment, and then concluded his remarks in a peculiarly penetrating voice:

"Under the circumstances, Mr. Capen, you cannot expect to fall back on us for recommendations." He paused. Donald bit his lips, bowed, and turned to go without a word. Robert Bohr followed him, continuing, "but if before the end of two months you decide to return and *conform to the methods of our house,* your old place will be open to you."

"Thank you," was the brief reply, and Donald passed out of the private office. His face was still pale as he began to put his desk in order. He carefully sorted his papers, throwing the useless ones into his waste-paper basket.

"Fired?" asked Greeley, succinctly.

"Yes."

"Whew! You *are* a guy! Up against another job now, hey?"

"I'll have to look for another job, of course."

Greeley watched curiously while Donald put the finishing touches to his desk, wiped it off, and started with his basket to the waste-paper box. Then Greeley turned to a gray-haired clerk, remarking, "Huh! I wouldn't slick up my desk so clean if I'd been fired!"

Robert Bohr, passing behind Greeley, overheard, and smiled inscrutably.

With a cordial clasp of the hand, Donald bade a regretful farewell to his new friends, and left the breezy, pleasant office to which he had come with high ambitions three months before.

From the shipping-house he went directly to his boarding-house, and climbed three flights of dimly lighted stairs to his room, overlooking the back yard. It was a dingy, uninviting room, but it was the only home he had. He sat down beside the table, rested his head on his hands, and thought.

He felt just then, despite his twenty-two years, the need of a mother to comfort him and of a father to advise. But he had neither—only the memory of those teachings, a part of which had caused this trouble.

His father's brother lived at the other side of the city, but Donald would not appeal to him again. It was through the uncle that he had obtained the position with Bohr Brothers.

In one corner of the room stood a rented typewriter. Donald had made himself its master by patient practice in the evenings. He was also learning stenography, in order to prove equal to any emergency which might arise in the office. He had invariably been the first to reach his desk in the morning and the last to leave at night. Quick, accurate, steady, he was rapidly making himself acquainted with the details of the business when—

"This is the way it all ends!" he muttered aloud.

After banking hours that afternoon Landis invaded the third-story room. Landis was a clerk in the Third National Bank. He did all that was required of him during banking hours, and did not weigh himself down with the responsibilities of that institution, either inside or outside its doors. Still, Landis was a good fellow, and had a genuine liking for Donald, whom he didn't understand.

"Now, Capen, what's the racket," he inquired, sitting on the edge of the bed. "Just met Greeley, and he said you'd been fired. Is it true?"

Donald nodded. He stood in front of his one window, staring at an assortment of high fences and waving clotheslines. "Yes, it's true," he admitted.

Landis threw one leg over the other. "Come out of your shell, old man, and tell me how it happened," he said.

Donald responded slowly: "It's like this, Landis. I—that is—back on the farm we never did unnecessary work on Sundays. My mother—" Donald stopped and swallowed, while the clotheslines blurred before his eyes.

"Yes, I understand," interposed the other, sympathetically.

"Well, with Bohr Brothers we're likely to be called to our desks any Sunday. At first when I saw the rush and commotion on the docks I supposed that the work was necessary—that the vessels were coming and then going on scheduled time; but I found out that whenever a cargo comes in Saturday night it is unloaded Sunday—not from necessity, but in order to get the cargo loaded and away one day earlier, and so make it more profitable. Yesterday I refused to work."

"But Greeley likes the Sunday work on account of the pay," interrupted Landis.

Donald nodded. "Yes, we're paid more than double."

"I shouldn't kick, then," said Landis, sagely.

"It's not a question of the money, and it's not a question of work, either. I've offered to work up till midnight any Saturday and begin at midnight any Sunday, but between these hours—" He turned abruptly to the window again.

"But see here, Capen," began Landis, from his height of superior wisdom and experience, "you must remember that you're not back on the farm. You can't carry such principles into business. Everything rushes here, and if you won't rush with the crowd you must expect to get fired right away. Better go easy on your notions and look out for number one."

Donald's eyes flushed and his lips tightened, until Landis

moved uncomfortably and hurried on: "I wish there was a place over at Third National, but we're full there."

He rose. "Say, what about that little excursion to Niagara that the fellows have planned for Friday evening?"

"I suppose you'll be obliged to count me out, as I'll be busy looking up another job."

"Well, if we must, we must, then. So long!" and Landis ran lightly down the stairs.

The following morning the search for work began, but didn't end. Day after day Donald tramped the streets of Buffalo, interviewing employers. Men liked his appearance, his quiet, straightforward manner, but the fact that Bohr Brothers, one of the best-known firms in the city, would give him no recommendation tipped the scale against him.

"Why were you discharged?" asked one merchant, favorably inclined toward the young man.

Donald told his story.

The merchant listened with a faint smile of unbelief, then said politely, "I'm sorry we have no place for you." To his stenographer, as Donald departed, he said, in a weary but audible tone, "What a cock-and-bull story! Won't recommend him, but want him back again! I should think he'd invent a better yarn!"

"I've got to start square, whatever I do!" Donald muttered, with the remark still in his ears. "If it does sound like a cock-and-bull story, it's the truth, and I'm not going to tell any other."

A month passed, and then one evening Greeley and Landis climbed the three flights to the upper hall of Donald's boarding-house, only to find him in still narrower quarters. He had moved into a tiny hall bedroom. Donald sat on the floor, Turk-fashion, leaving the narrow bed to Landis and the small chair for Greeley.

"What luck?" asked Greeley.

"None."

"Then," began Greeley, casting a triumphant glance at Landis, "you'll be ready to come back when I tell you the old man hasn't forgotten that he wants you."

"Wants you!" chimed in Landis. "Well, I should say so, after fixing things so you couldn't get a place readily anywhere else! That plan of refusing recommendations and holding the place open is a slick one to drive you back. I tell you, Bohr has a smart head on him!"

Donald made no response.

"Well, I came up to tell you the latest, Capen," Greeley went on. "The old man stopped at my desk this morning, and asked where you were and what you were doing. When I told him, he snapped his fingers and said, 'Idiot! We intended to give him a raise next month.' After he had gone on, he came back and added, 'Just tell him from me that one month is already gone.'"

"Another raise next month!" cried Landis, excitedly. "And you've had one already! I tell you what, it wouldn't take *me* long to decide in your place. Why, man alive"—Landis leaned over and slapped Donald's shoulder—"you were simply walking up the ladder there!"

"You're right he was!" Greeley interposed, heartily. "He'd already gone ahead of some of the men who'd been in the office for years."

That night Donald didn't sleep well, but the following morning he stepped out on the street with the light of a new resolve in his eyes. His money was failing, while his board bills remained the same, and the idea of going into debt never occurred to him. His father had regarded debt with a horror which had impressed the son. Therefore, while looking for a position suited to his education and ability, Donald had determined on a course which hurt his pride. He reported to the foreman of a gang of laborers, shouldered a pick, and began work on an excavation just back of the Third National Bank.

In overalls and shirt, he dug on steadily day after day, as he had driven his pen in Bohr Brothers' office. The boss liked him. "He keeps at it whether I'm lookin' or not," he informed two gentlemen, who stood one day before an open window in the basement of the Third National. One of the men was the president of the bank.

That evening Greeley ran up to Donald's hall bedroom. Greeley was in a hurry to join the boys, and didn't have time to sit down. Donald had ceased to join the boys.

"See here, Capen," cried Greeley, breathlessly, "I just dropped up to warn you that you've got only one day left of those two months! I tell you, when the old man says a thing it goes. But the Bohrs want you back bad, and don't you forget it. Robert stalked over to my desk today, and wanted to know if I supposed that young fool knew what a good business chance he was throwing away. Who knows but you might land in the firm yet if you came back?"

Donald had risen and faced Greeley. He appeared older than when he left the office. His hands were hardened and his face burned, but the expression of determination about his mouth had deepened.

"Greeley," he said, in even tones, "I'm not going back."

Greeley became agitated. He ran his fingers through his hair and gesticulated excitedly.

"I think, Capen, it's time you woke up. You're throwing away the chance of a lifetime."

"Very well," said Donald.

There was a brief pause, then Greeley swung on his heel. "Well, I give up on you!" he said, in an annoyed tone, and ran downstairs.

Donald stood beside the window a few moments, his forehead contracted. It was not the first time he had faced the temptation to drop the pick and take up the pen, to stop moving upstream, and drift down into an easy place, with good pay and every chance to rise. Why not? Why should he be burdened with principles which were millstones hung about his neck?

Presently he shook himself impatiently and began brushing his hat. The world was wide, and he was young and hopeful. "If I'm square with myself," he said aloud, "I'll succeed sometime, somehow. Anyway, I cannot give up," and he started out on his nightly quest for better employment.

As he turned into Main Street he came face to face with Robert Bohr and a stranger. He raised his hat with a clear, direct glance at the former, and was passing on, when, to his surprise, Mr. Bohr stopped and accosted him.

"Shall I find you at your desk in the morning?" The question came abruptly.

Donald's eyes were steady. "No, sir."

The stranger, who had stepped beyond the two, turned and glanced at Donald with interest.

"Tomorrow is the last day you can return," persisted Bohr. "After that the place is closed to you. I never go back on my word."

"Neither do I, sir," said Donald.

The following morning, under the hot sun, he began work as usual behind the Third National Bank. Rain had fallen during the night, and his boots and overalls were soon heavy with mud, while drops of muddy water splashed up into his face. A mile away, a desk awaited him in a long, pleasant room, while the breeze from the lake swept in.

At the thought, he struck his pick into a mass of splintered rock as if he were burying the thought of that desk where it would never again rise to trouble him.

"Hello, Capen!" sounded a familiar voice behind him. It was an excited voice, and Donald turned in astonishment, to find Landis picking his way gingerly through the mud. "Hey, there!" cried Landis. "You're wanted in the bank right away!"

The point of Donald's pick fell harmlessly among the stones as he turned and surveyed Landis.

"You're wanted by the president," Landis repeated.

"*Me!*" exclaimed Donald.

"Yes, you."

"What for?"

"I don't know. Make tracks, now! He's waiting for you."

Past rows of men, who stared in frank amazement at the muddied workman, Donald passed into the handsomely furnished private office of the bank president, whom he found alone.

The banker was a middle-aged, gray-haired man, whose pleasant face puzzled Donald. *Where have I seen him before?* he thought, as the president rose and offered his hand, saying cordially:

"I'm glad Mr. Landis found you so soon, Mr. Capen."

"Thank you," Donald replied, looking down at his dirty overalls. "I was obliged to come as I was."

"Exactly as I expected you to come. Will you sit down?"

Donald glanced at the softly upholstered chair behind him, and shook his head with a smile. "No, thank you."

The president's eyes twinkled. "What I have to say, Mr. Capen, can be said briefly," he began. "I wish to offer you a position in this bank."

Donald couldn't believe he had heard aright. He opened his mouth, but no sound came. Finally he gasped:

"In *this* bank?"

The president seemed to enjoy his amazement. "Yes," he said. "As soon as you are fitted for the work we shall make you receiving-teller."

The blur which had come before Donald's eyes suddenly cleared. He knew now where he'd seen the president. Last evening with Bohr! How much of his record with the Bohr Brothers did the man before him know? Donald bent his head in troubled thought. When he spoke, an instant later, he was really thinking aloud: "It's best to start square."

"Yes," said the president, gravely, "it's always best to start square."

Donald drew a long breath and told his story. When he finished, the president was smiling again.

"You haven't told it all," he remarked.

Donald's eyes opened in astonishment. "What——" he began; but the other interrupted.

"After your dismissal you arranged your desk as carefully as if you'd been granted a vacation on full pay."

Donald passed his hand in bewilderment across his forehead. "How do you know?" he asked.

The president reached forward, selected a sheet of note paper, and pointed to the printed list of the officers of the bank heading the sheet. His own name came first, followed by "Richard Bohr, Vice-President."

Donald read the name aloud in a dazed voice, adding, "I don't understand."

"My boy," said the president, quietly, "we've been watching you these two months. The business world is looking out for young men of action and brains, who can stand by their principles in the face of financial inducements to the contrary. Robert Bohr thinks—the board of trustees of this bank think—that it is safe to entrust other people's money to the care of such a man."

Nothing is known of ANNIE LOUISE LEE *except that she wrote for turn-of-the-twentieth-century inspirational and family magazines.*

OCTOBER SONG

Joseph Leininger Wheeler

1

Oh to be in New England in autumn
When the leaves turn from green to gold;
Oh to be in New England in autumn
When I too am growing old.

The years, they are a-passing
Passing like the scarlet, brown, and umber leaves
Wearily letting go, and cascading down
From the soon to be naked trees.

Rolling up the rugged shore are waves of blue and gray;
Blue today in the serenity of Indian Summer,
Gray tomorrow in the hurricanes of late autumn
With autumn leaves the in-between.

For I too am nearing my October;
Remorselessly the sands in my hourglass

Sift down and down and down
Just like the leaves, just like the leaves.

Oh heart! Just like the leaves.

Pardon me, is this your scarf?"

"Oh, thank you, yes! How irresponsible of me."

"Well, I don't know about that—the wind's pretty strong this morning."

"You're right. Do you think it might be blowing up a storm?"

"Could be. Heard on the news that a big one is flexing its muscles out in mid-Atlantic."

"Hope it holds off for a while before it comes this way."

"Yeah, that would kind of ruin your vacation—you *are* on vacation?"

"Yes, but that's not what I mean. I love storms."

"Oh?"

"You'll think it selfish of me, but since I'm on a bus tour—up here to ride the colors down—I don't want to see the leaves fall this soon."

"Don't blame you. Spectacular this year, aren't they?"

"Yes, but I can't compare them with other years, as this is my first time."

"First time in New England?"

"No, first time to be here in the fall. And what about *you?*"

He paused at length and mentally traveled through the long years before answering, "I'm afraid that would be a long story."

Suddenly she looked down at her watch and sprang to her feet in alarm: "Oh my, it's quarter to eight! Bus leaves in fifteen minutes. Gotta run."

"Where are you heading today?"

"Kennebunkport."

"So am I," he said. It was true, although he hadn't planned on getting there so soon. But for some strange reason his plans had changed.

"What a coincidence."

"Yes, it is, isn't it?"

And so it began…

———

At the venerable Shawmut Inn, they greeted each other that night with the ease of old friends. Since the inn was filled to capacity, it took some time to get a table, and so they had plenty of time to talk.

"So, what about that 'long story' you spoke of in Gloucester?" she started in.

"Oh—I'd really rather hear yours first."

"Well, I don't think you'll find my life very interesting—it certainly won't take long to tell. But give me a few moments to get my thoughts together."

As he watched her pucker up that still creamy forehead, his mind missed nothing: *She intrigues me. About five-nine, I'd guess. Clairol brunette—probably graying beneath. Fiftyish. Trim. Good figure. Healthy—takes good care of herself. Laugh lines in her face. In fact, I love her laugh; it's so infectious—low toned, in a sort of pleasant minor key. Don't think I could ever tire of hearing it. But there are pain lines in her face too—she's known trouble. Attractive, probably a beauty in her thirties. Good eye for clothes and color; well-groomed, too. Intelligent. Verbal. Wonder what kind of a story she'll have to tell.*

Unbeknown to him, behind her long eyelashes she was arriving at conclusions of her own: *I like his virile ruggedness. Reminds me of a Clint Eastwood character, although I doubt that this man could ever be ruthless. Probably six-two. Salt-and-pepper gray. Physically fit. Dresses casually but well. Laugh lines and pain lines, with pain predominating—I'm guessing his life has been anything but easy. Thinks more than he talks. A man of distinction who would stand out anywhere. I'd like to know him better.*

Their observations were cut short when a waiter indicated that their table near the fireplace was ready. The candlelight illuminated her inner radiance, almost taking his breath away. *She's truly lovely. Candlelight has this trick of stripping away the years—but only if a woman is tender and kind inside; if she's not, candlelight can do nothing to soften that inner hardness.*

Eventually, he managed to draw out her story. But it wasn't easy, and it didn't flow. Born and raised in Virginia's Shenandoah Valley—*Aha! I knew she was from the South!*—her father a banker, her mother a stay-at-home mom. No siblings. Majored in psych at the University of Virginia; graduate work at Duke. A marriage. A number of positions here and there, always with people—she loved people. Then a move to the Big Apple, and up the corporate ladder of a large telecommunications firm.

"Then…" her account came sputtering to an end, and she nearly lost her composure. Clearly she didn't want to go on, but she gamely managed anyhow. "Well, it's hard to relive this part of my story, the wounds are so fresh. It…it just happened two weeks ago."

"Oh?"

"Well, I certainly don't mean to imply that it was a surprise. We *all* knew it was coming—the merger, that is—and then it hit the newsstands before it was announced to us. *That* hurt. And though we were three times as big—I still can't figure out how such a thing can be!—we turned out to be the swallow*ee* instead of the swallow*er*. For a time we thought the changes would be minor ones—that's what we'd been told. But three weeks ago, they started calling us in one at a time, at fifteen-minute intervals. I hope never in my life to face another week like that one. We all aged years waiting for the ax to fall. Some—a very small number—were retained; most were not. It was Thursday at 11:30 A.M. before they got to me. I saw the news on their faces before a word was said. After sixteen years with that company, and for the first time ever, I was without a job. I felt the floor of my life collapse under me. It was as if I were in a free fall into the unknown."

"I trust they offered you a good severance package?"

"So-so. I wasn't high enough on the corporate ladder to get a silver parachute, which my boss did. He got a check for five million and eight million in stock. *His* boss, the CEO, got a golden parachute, ten times that. Mine was only copper, enough to pay off a few credit cards and six payments on my condo mortgage."

"*My*...mortgage?"

Wincing, but looking him full in the face, she repeated: "*My* mortgage—and enough to give me some time off before returning to New York to look for another job."

"So, how did you, uh—"

"How did I get *here?*" Her eyes twinkled in remembrance. "Well, I'd always wanted to be in New England in the fall—October is my favorite month of the year. The timing of my...uh... termination...was perfect. My travel agent was able to get me on this tour—since there was a last-minute cancellation—and here I am!"

With equally perfect timing, the waiter chose this moment to bring their food.

After asking if they needed anything else, he left.

There was an awkward pause, a silence neither seemed to know how to break. It was he who finally did:

"Do you mind if I ask a blessing?"

"Why no, I'd like that," she answered in pleased surprise.

"Dear Lord, here we are, two strangers in the process of becoming friends. Bless this food and our association together, we pray. In Thy name. Amen."

He guided their dialogue away from personal things and toward the corporate world and mind-set she had so recently departed. Every time she tried to steer the conversation back to the personal, he deftly deflected it. Thus she finished her meal and got up from the table without knowing anything about him but his name: John. John A. Baldwin. Hers, he learned, was Eve, short for Evangeline: Eve LeBlanc.

She didn't even lift an eyebrow when he mentioned that he, too, was planning on staying in the lovely seacoast village of Boothbay the next night. After all, she hadn't heard *his* story yet. And although she didn't yet know why, she was strongly drawn to this stranger with intense eyes, broad shoulders, and a spring in his step.

Yes, he was nice looking, but that alone could not possibly account for the attraction. She sensed a deeper reason—a strength of character, a powerful sense of purpose she had never observed in a man before.

2

The twilight is sad and cloudy,
> The wind blows wild and free,
And like the wings of sea-birds
> Flash the white caps of the sea.

But in the fisherman's cottage
    There shines a ruddier light,
And a little face at the window
    Peers out into the night.

Close, close it pressed to the window,
    As if those childish eyes
Were looking into the darkness,
    To see some form arise.

And a woman's waving shadow
    Is passing to and fro,
Now rising to the ceiling,
    Now bowing and bending low.

What tale do the roaring ocean,
    And the night-wind, bleak and wild,
As they beat at the crazy casement,
    Tell to that little child?

And why do the roaring ocean,
    And the night-wind, wild and bleak,
As they beat at the heart of the mother,
    Drive the colour from her cheek?
        —"Twilight," by Henry Wadsworth Longfellow

Late afternoon shadows were long by the time John and Eve walked across the lawn of old Spruce Point Inn, dazzling white against the green of lawn and trees and the bronze-blue of the sea. Approaching a rustic bench, they shared the silence broken only by the lapping wavelets and raucous *ca-ca-cawing* of the gulls. Then, out of the harbor came a sleek windjammer, relic of a bygone age, slowly gliding through the channel. Only after intently watching the tall ship until it was well out to sea did John tell his story.

"I was born in that old fishing town of Gloucester, made famous by Kipling's *Captains Courageous*. My father was a fishing-boat captain, and Mother stayed home with me. Every time Dad's schooner put out to sea, we'd watch it until it disappeared on the horizon, just as we did a few moments ago. Then, at home, many times during the day and far into the evening, we'd scan the horizon."

"Oh, I know what you're talking about!" Eve interrupted. "I saw it when we were staying at Bass Rocks in Gloucester—the 'captain's walk,' they called it, but some called it 'widow's walk' because—" she saw his face and sputtered to a halt.

"Yes," he nodded, "that's what we called it. We lived on that Twin Lights beach, and not far out is the reef of Norman's Woe. Dad used to read Longfellow's 'The Wreck of the Hesperus' to us—Mom could never bear to read it. It was too close to home, she said." He recited a passage.

> "It was the schooner *Hesperus*
>   That sailed the wintry sea;
> And the skipper had taken his little daughter
>   To bear him company."

He paused. "Always loved that poem—sent chills up my spine every time though."

Spontaneously, Eve picked up many stanzas later:

> "Such was the wreck of the *Hesperus*,
>   In the midnight and the snow!

Christ save us all from a death like this,
On the reef of Norman's Woe!"

Startled, he stared at her. "You know Longfellow too?"

"Raised on him."

"Well, I declare."

"Yes, my mother knew much of Longfellow by heart. Trained me to follow in her footsteps." She laughed. "Not much of a call for elocutionists these days."

"More's the pity."

"But pardon me, John; I interrupted your story."

"Well," he continued slowly, "it was this time of year. I was eight, and Dad was out to sea. One of the most terrible hurricanes ever to hit this coast struck that year. Mom had a premonition and clung to Dad's arm that autumn morning, crying almost uncontrollably—only time I ever heard her do such a thing—*begging* him to cancel the fishing venture. He looked at her sadly and said, 'Mary, you know I can't stay here. If I did, how would we pay our bills?' Eventually she calmed down and bravely kissed him good-bye. But that night I heard her sobbing in her room."

After pausing for control, he resumed. "Weather forecasting was pretty primitive in those days, so the nor'easter took us by surprise. At first it was only the wind, then came rain, then lightning. Then came what seemed the end of the world."

Again, he was momentarily unable to continue. Eve sat there mute, knowing without being told, the rest of the story.

"Dad never came back, but the wreckage of his schooner washed up on the beach some two hundred miles north of here."

"Oh!" was all that Eve could say. Finally she asked, "And your mother?"

When John spoke again his voice was flat, devoid of emotion:

"My mother was all cried out long before word of the wreckage reached Gloucester. She *knew* Dad's ship could never have survived that storm. She still turned white when old Captain Mindock brought her the news. Next morning she looked twenty years older. Never a day had passed without her lilting singing until Dad left the harbor that last time. She never sang again. She was a one-man woman. Mother died five weeks later—of a broken heart."

"Oh!"

He stopped now. They parted soon after without discussing her tour itinerary.

———

Next evening Eve was sitting in the Camden Deli, looking out the window with unseeing eyes. Below the deli, the Megunticook River cascaded down into the harbor.

Suddenly a tall figure stood beside her and asked, "Mind if I join you?" And in answer to her lifted eyebrows confessed, "A generous tip to your bus driver."

The light came back to her eyes as she pointed to a chair and smiled. She had never expected to see him again.

They did not leave their table until night had fallen and not until he had told her "the rest of the story."

With his father and mother both dead and debts exceeding assets, the numbed child had been launched upon the sea of unwantedness. Several relatives had concluded that blood was blood and felt obligated to take him in, but that didn't mean they had to like it. Dreary days, weeks, months, and years passed as he shuttled from house to house, little more than an unpaid servant, without a place to call home, a school to attend, or worse yet, no one to put an arm around him or tell him he was loved.

At age fifteen he overheard his Uncle Jacob say to his wife: "I'm sick and tired of taking care of Johnny, and so are my brothers. What do you say we put him in a foster home?"

That was enough. Not staying to hear her answer, John tossed his few personal belongings into his battered suitcase and sneaked out the back door shortly after midnight. He had no idea where he would go. He only knew he had to get away, and far, and fast.

He hopped a westbound freight train just as daylight broke. The only money to his name was a wrinkled and long-hoarded dollar bill and forty-three cents. He wasn't discovered until just as the train was slowing down for Buffalo. But luck was with him. A kindhearted brakeman with boys of his own listened to John's story with a sympathetic heart and gave him ten dollars, a handful of meal tickets, and a train pass to San Francisco.

"And what did you do *there?*" Eve asked.

"Well, since all I knew was the sea, I signed on as a cabin boy for the SS *Manchuria,* on the Orient route. Six years later, on coming of age, I disembarked for the last time at Fisherman's Wharf."

He'd had plenty of time to think during those six years, think about what he wanted to do with his life. By that time he'd read through entire libraries, attempting to gain the education he'd never received. Having lived frugally, he left the ship with a nest egg of almost five thousand dollars.

A long, hard road followed. He worked at any job he could find to earn money for college tuition and living expenses, and he usually took but one class at a time.

"For how long?" she asked.

"Fourteen years," he answered. "Graduated with a master's in history from UC Berkeley."

"And what then?"

"Well, I decided to try my hand at writing. I had neither the time nor the inclination to date, so I was free of marital or family obligations. I had no roots. Twenty years of my life had gone by since Mom died, and I had been deprived of my childhood, adolescence, and youth—I never had any opportunity to play.

"How sad!"

"Yes, but I've made up for it since."

"Oh?"

"After graduation, I headed up Highway 1 on the California coast, just to think. A lot of people were frying their brains with drugs during those days—hippies were everywhere—so another beach bum didn't cause so much as a ripple of interest."

Eve smiled.

"I kept going north. Ran out of money near Coos Bay, Oregon. Got a job in a mill there. Camped out in a KOA. Stayed until I had a nest egg, then moved on. That became the pattern of my life."

"You mean wander then work, wander then work?"

"Exactly."

"Were you writing?"

"No, only journaling. I didn't feel ready for writing yet. Not for real people."

She laughed. "You mean your university professors weren't real people?"

"Not really—they spoke only stodgy educationese. I had to unlearn that. Nobody voluntarily reads educationese unless they're mighty hard up for something to do."

"You may be right about that."

"I decided to hit the road and get to know real people in real places before I tried to write professionally. But journaling was a must. Writers like Robert Louis Stevenson and Zane Grey filled their journals with their daily observations, thoughts, discussions with people they met, and physical descriptions of the country, buildings, weather, wildlife, and people. Years later they could step backward in time and place and write like they were *there*."

"Brilliant concept!"

"Well, it has worked for me—over time."

"Over how much time?"

"Let me see, I was about forty before I started writing short pieces for publication. Been at it ever since."

"And your settings?"

"Everywhere. I've traveled the world, but my heartland is North America, especially New England, although I've driven clear to the southernmost tip of South America!"

"Clear to the Straits of Magellan?"

"Yep."

"What a trip that must have been!"

"Yes, because it was on a shoestring budget. Many years went by before I did more than break even. More than twenty, in fact."

"*So...*you're in your sixties. You don't look it."

"You're so kind. Perhaps it's because youth is more a state of mind than a chronological thing. Some people are *born* old, and others never do get old."

"Intriguing. Care to elaborate?"

"Let's see. I feel that children are adaptable, resilient, don't know the meaning of the word *stranger*, gobble up knowledge and life with all the intensity of a starving person. They are willing to try anything, they are filled with a sense of wonder about life— that's why Christ declared that except we become as little children again, we'll never make it into the kingdom."

"Sobering thought."

"True. So, I have been a veritable Don Quixote, jousting at the windmills of life."

"But success has come to you now?"

"Moderate success. I'm no household word. I'm not on the talk-show circuit. And I'm glad about that."

"How's that? Wouldn't you like to be a celebrity?"

"No. It costs too much."

"Huh?"

"How shall I put it? I know. It's this way: Being a celebrity is almost the worst thing that could happen to an author. For several reasons. First of all, you lose your ability to get honest answers from people you interview—if they've seen you on TV and in the tabloids, they either clam up or sugarcoat what they tell you. They lose their naturalness."

"Hmm. I see how that could be true."

"Yes. But it's more than that. Celebrity writers sell their privacy for money and can't go anywhere without being recognized and lionized. Everything they do or say is public record. And not being a saint, that would be hard on me."

"Hard on *anyone,* I'd think."

"But there's even more to this fame thing. It has built into it the seeds of its own destruction."

"How's that?"

"Well, I know I'm probably in the minority in the writing community, as secular as it is today, but I feel strongly that all creativity comes from God. All concepts worth listening to, that is. That's why the secret of creativity is humility, the recognition that wisdom comes from only one source: God, not self. That's why I pray the prayer of Solomon every day."

"Solomon—I'm a bit hazy on the story—prayed for wisdom?"

"Yes, when he became king of Israel, God asked him what gift he most wanted. He answered that being a king terrified him. Wisdom was the gift he yearned for. God gave it to him, making him the 'wisest man who ever lived,' other than Christ, of course. So I feel terrified, too, at the prospect of writing things that people might read anywhere around the world—and perhaps a hundred years, a thousand years from now. Certainly Homer had no idea people would still be reading him thousands of years later."

"So you are afraid of your ego?"

"Most certainly! When an author succumbs to the sin of pride, his doom as a great author is already sealed. And it's so difficult not to. When you see all those people standing in line to get your squiggly lines on their books, that insidious deception rises within you again: *I must be something pretty special. I've really arrived!* I'm convinced that once you begin dwelling on success, you're on your way down. The only way to stay truly successful is to remain humble and teachable. Christ spoke about pride often."

"You think about God a lot, don't you?"

"Yes. Without God, life has no meaning whatsoever."

"I agree with you."

"I was hoping that you would."

"Why?"

"Because I'd like to know you better, and we could never become more than just friends if you didn't share this relationship with my Lord."

"Are you getting serious, John?"

"Afraid I am. And I don't have much time left."

"I don't really know what you mean by that, but if you're getting serious, I'm very sorry to hear it."

"Why?"

"Because I'm not."

"Why?"

"*Why?* Because I've been terribly burned."

"I was wondering when you'd get around to the rest of your story."

"Guess this is as good a time as any. I was married for only six months many years ago. Married to one I believed was my soul mate. He...he walked out on me one bright spring morning and never came back."

"Give any reasons?"

"Of course! Many. In short, I just wasn't a free enough spirit for him."

"Meaning?"

"That he had no room for God and Christian values in his life."

"And you hadn't known he felt that way earlier?"

"Yes," she said slowly, drawing the word out as she considered it, "but I had hoped his love for me would deepen his love for God."

"Mighty dangerous assumption. Although people have been making that deadly mistake since almost the dawn of time."

"How can you be so sure?"

"How can you *not* see the truth in it, you foolish woman?"

"How dare you call me that!"

"But it's true! You've let one bad experience poison your entire life! Just because you married a man you had no business marrying, and he walked out on you, is no reason to condemn *all* men. Look at it this way—"

"I don't have to look at it *any* way, Mr. Know-It-All! Who are you to be telling me how to think or behave? This relationship isn't going anywhere—*ever!*"

And she stood up, avoided his eyes, and stalked out of the room.

3

You cannot put a Fire out—
A thing that can ignite
Can go, itself, without a Fan—
Upon the slowest Night—

You cannot fold a Flood—
And put it in a Drawer—
Because the Winds would find it out—
And tell your Cedar Floor.
   —"You Cannot Put a Fire Out,"
    by Emily Dickinson

Next day the bus pulled out early, for they were heading inland to catch the colors at their peak. Eve was miserable without really knowing why. It had happened again, as it had so many times before. She would let a relationship get to the stage where she began to genuinely care for the person and, as certain as dawn and dusk, she'd find some way to sabotage it. No doubt she'd wrecked this one, too.

Outside her window like an ever-rolling diorama ran New England in autumn: Leaves of gold, scarlet, brown, and green; ocean, rivers, creeks, and lakes of blue, gray, and seafoam; stark white church steeples spearing the azure sky; smoke and flames rising from burning leaves; signs advertising apple cider and maple sugar; and vistas of mountain ranges undulating into infinity—all this, tinctured by the mellow softness of Indian Summer autumn: the sense of Autumn's reluctance to leave and of Winter's reluctance to step in. Waiting...the prevailing theme.

As the kaleidoscope of colors whirled past her window, it all began to blur as she considered that *he* would not be there at the end of the day. Why she cared, she didn't really know. She only knew that there was an empty spot inside her that had not been there before. She didn't even know his address, phone number, fax, or e-mail. Fleetingly she wondered if he even had a home. He didn't know how to reach her either, and he didn't have the rest of her itinerary—at least not from her.

She comforted herself by thinking, *Well, I was right and he was dead wrong! How was I to know all this when Walter told me before the wedding that he'd be a Christian for my sake? In fact,* he promised *me! Of course all men are like Walter. After all, beneath the skin, aren't all men the same?* But somehow she was no longer as certain of this simplistic generalization as she'd been before.

Late in the afternoon they reached Derry, New Hampshire. On the mike at the front of the bus, the tour guide filled them in on the life and times of Robert Frost, who once lived and wrote here. Though little of his life story was new to her, she found herself looking forward to seeing that farm. Finally, down the leaf-strewn street, there it was, just as she'd pictured it in her mind: plain, modest in size, and glorified by the golden-mantled trees rimming the pasture.

After touring the house and adjacent barn, which now housed memorabilia, she walked down the path the poet had so loved. Near the first corner, she stopped and sat down on a bench. With her was her well-marked anthology of Frost's poetry. Off to her right was the famed "mending wall," looking ever so much smaller than she'd imagined it. She recited from memory—"Before I built

a wall I'd ask to know / What I was walling in or walling out"—
and was jolted by the realization that just last night she had built a
wall. Now she wondered whether it had been intended to wall in
or wall out. Or both.

In her mind's eye she could envision the feeble old hired man
Silas, who many years before had come to this very farmhouse to
die. He had come here with—she found the lines—"And nothing
to look backward to with pride / And nothing to look forward to
with hope." To be completely honest with herself, was she any better off in this respect than old Silas?

Scanning the poem, she came to one of the most poignant
couplets in the English language: "Home is the place where, when
you have to go there, / They have to take you in."

Did she really have a home? Oh, her cookie-cutter condo
didn't really count: a home represented shared dreams. When she
died, who would miss her? Who would really care? Her passing
would leave hardly a ripple behind—nothing at all like what John's
would, with his writings. But *why*, she now asked herself, this new
feeling of low self-worth? After all, she'd only lost a job and could
easily find another. Suddenly she had an epiphany: *All these years
I've ridiculed men for their silly way of doubting their self-worth
just because they were passed over for promotion or got fired from
a job. Men are so dumb that way! Now, here I am doing the very
same thing: I'm employed, so I'm special; I'm fired, so I'm a failure!
Even though I know it's a fallacy, I still buy into it. Heaven help me!
How John would laugh at me for such illogical reasoning. Now why in
the world am I thinking about that man again? And why do I dwell so
much on being alone? It never bothered me before. Much.*

Her tour group stayed the night in Amherst, Massachusetts,
famous the world over because a recluse once lived here, a never-
married woman who rarely stirred from her house. All the life the

woman knew wended its way down the dusty street in front of her house. *Tomorrow I'll see this woman's entire world—imagine!*

But Eve's excitement paled when she got off the bus, and *he* was not there. She did not sleep well that night.

Next morning their group wedged themselves into the narrow stairway of the house in which America's greatest poetess, Emily Dickinson, had lived. Several years before, Eve had read Dickinson clear through, so somehow, in visiting Amherst, she had a sense of homecoming. She wondered, as have so many others, why Dickinson never married. In the little gift shop were Dickinson poems suitable for framing. One caught her eye:

> Go not too near a House of Rose—
> The depredation of a Breeze
> Or inundation of a Dew
> Alarms its walls away—
>
> Nor try to tie the Butterfly,
> Nor climb the Bars of Ecstasy,
> In insecurity to lie
> Is Joy's insuring quality.
>   —"Go Not Too Near a House of Rose"

Suddenly it struck her: All her life she'd been demanding security as a precondition to commitment. And here Dickinson had postulated that only in insecurity can joy be fully savored. *Security—isn't the very word a travesty? There* is *no real security on this planet.*

They stayed at White River Junction that night.

The next day was a full one, with many stops en route to Crawford Notch and the great hotel in Bretton Woods, under the shadow of towering Mount Washington, now iridescently ablaze with light. Eve had always loved old hotels and inns; in their rooms she had a sense of the past meeting the present, and she couldn't help wondering who'd gone to sleep in her assigned room in years gone by.

She was looking out the great window in the lobby when clouds closed in. Rain began to fall softly. Withdrawing to the welcome warmth of the fireplace, she continued to stare out into the rain, which now fell harder. The wind began to intensify. Lines from Longfellow dropped into her consciousness from days gone by:

> The day is cold, and dark, and dreary;
> It rains, and the wind is never weary;
> The vine still clings to the mouldering walls,
> But at every gust the dead leaves fall,
>   And the day is dark and dreary.
>
> My life is cold, and dark, and dreary;
> It rains, and the wind is never weary;
> My thoughts still cling to the mouldering Past,
> But the hopes of youth fall thick in the blast,
>   And the days are dark and dreary.
>
> Be still, sad heart! and cease repining;
> Behind the clouds is the sun still shining;
> Thy fate is the common fate of all,
> Into each life some rain must fall,
>   Some days must be dark and dreary.
>   —"The Rainy Day"

Somewhat comforted by the last stanza, she wandered aimlessly into the hotel gift shop in search of a good read. Overhearing the manager talking to a guest about a new book, she drew near and shamelessly eavesdropped.

"You haven't heard of him? Where have you *been?* He's one of New England's own, though goodness knows he's not here much anymore. But though his world has become much bigger than New England, he's never forgotten his roots. This is his new book, *October Song.* It's a mixture of poetry and prose, and living proof that his heart remains here. If you can get that opening stanza of his lead poem out of your head, you'll be doing better than I, for it haunts me."

Without bothering to even look at the book, Eve asked the manager to bag one up for her. Back in her room, she put on her nightgown, snuggled down in the antique bed, and reached for her latest purchase. Halfway from the nightstand, Eve's arm froze in midair: On the cover of the book, in large letters, was the byline:

By John A. Baldwin

Each stop since Camden had been a revelation to Eve: a revelation in terms of who she really was, who John was, and life itself. She was not the same woman she had been only days before. She looked back at her harsh words and walking out of John's presence and life as the act of someone she neither knew nor liked, and at his stern words that had triggered her temper tantrum as being exactly what she'd been needing for a long, long time. Now on this stormy night, she was willing—*eager*—to read what he might have to say about life and, indirectly, about himself.

About halfway through the book her eyes were arrested by lines having to do with troubles and hard times:

God permits troubles to come our way in order to strengthen us. Only during trauma do we grow, do our roots grope their way deep down through earth and stone in order to survive the storms that periodically assail us. There are no exceptions: No tree ever became strong in a hothouse.

In this respect, many years ago I made a pilgrimage to Craigie House, Longfellow's lovely home in Cambridge. The guide that day was exceptional, and had the unique ability of making each of us feel we knew Longfellow personally before we left. He recited from memory a number of his poems, one of them being "Rainy Day." Perhaps because it was raining hard as he recited it, and perhaps because my life has included so many rainy days (metaphorically speaking), I strongly identified with the persona of the poem, especially with the recurring line, "Cold, dark, and dreary."

The guide pointed out that this poem came straight from the heart, that when the poet wrote of pain and trouble, he knew firsthand whereof he wrote. He told us how Longfellow's sister Elizabeth, whom he loved dearly, died young. Shortly after he had taken his bride to Europe, while studying in Holland, a child was born to them. Their joy turned to heartbreak as the baby weakened and died. His young wife, devastated and inconsolable, pined away and died as well.

As if all that wasn't enough tragedy for a lifetime, not long after his second marriage, to beautiful Frances Appleton, they lost their first child, Fanny, who embodied all the sweetness that had been taken from him earlier.

Before continuing his story, our guide took us into the library, where Longfellow wrote, and it was here in this setting that he told us of an event he could never relate without tears.

It had been a hot July day, and Frances, in an effort to make her two little girls more comfortable in the oppressive heat, had just cut off their curls, and was carefully placing them in two little packages and sealing them for safekeeping. Somehow, thanks to a dropped match or a piece of the burning wax, her light muslin dress caught fire, and instantly she was a living torch. With a heartrending cry of terror, she ran to her husband in the library. All his attempts to extinguish the flames in time proved futile, and his lovely wife died the next day. She was buried on their wedding anniversary, a wreath of orange blossoms in her hair. Longfellow had been so severely burned himself trying to save her that he could not even attend her funeral.

Eighteen years later, on their anniversary day, he penned one of the most moving poems our language knows. So intensely personal was the subject that he kept it in his personal papers—apparently, he never intended it to be published. It was discovered in his private papers a number of years after his death. One of his wife's favorite pictures depicted a mountain in Colorado, Mount Holy Cross, which has on its face two deep crevices intersecting in the shape of a huge cross. So deep are they that the sun's summer rays cannot penetrate the snow resting in them. Drawing from this, and the anguish that never, never would leave him, he wrote these heartfelt words:

> In the long sleepless watches of the night,
> A gentle face—the face of one long dead—

Looks at me from the wall, where round
        its head
The night-lamp casts a halo of pale light
Here in this room she died; and soul more white
        Never through martyrdom of fire was led
        To its repose; nor can in books be read
        The legend of a life more benedight.
There is a mountain in the distant West
        That, sun-defying, in its deep ravines
        Displays a cross of snow upon its side.
Such is the cross I wear upon my breast
        These eighteen years, through all the
                changing scenes
        And seasons, changeless since the day
                she died.
                        —"The Cross of Snow"

After returning to my room that night, I thought, *what
if all this had happened to me? Would I, like Longfellow, have
picked up the jagged pieces of my life and tried to make some
sort of sense of them? Look at what the man became, in spite
of—or perhaps because of—all this: the most beloved poet
America has ever known. More beloved even than Robert Frost,
for Longfellow was never mean-spirited.*

I determined that if Longfellow could put all this behind
him and bravely face life, the least I could do would be to
follow his example, I who had suffered far less than he.

Knowing what John *had* suffered made Eve respect him even more
for downplaying his own sorrows.

Eve then turned back to the first section of the book, and read again:

I have always loved Autumn in New England, and so I try to meet my tryst with her every year. Two songs have deeply moved me since I was young. They are Johnny Mercer's "Autumn Leaves" and Kurt Weill's "September Song." They move me still, even more than they did in those days gone by, perhaps because those words now mirror me, and my age.

For me, too, the days are "dwindling down to a precious few." I, too, no longer have time for the "waiting game." I, too, have reached my life's September, and October is knocking at my door. And well I know how great a distance separates May from December.

But I don't feel old. Like Tennyson's immortal Ulysses, I am nowhere near ready to slow my wandering steps and wait until Death comes after me. Death is going to pant a little before he catches me. As long as I live and breathe, I shall create and attempt to make a difference. I shall grow, learn, and ever hone my craft. I shall stay young till that last breath. Just as the sea refuses to surrender, but assaults its beaches millennium after millennium, just so I refuse to surrender or slow down. Who knows, perhaps love may yet come to me, improbable as it may seem after so many fruitless years of searching for "the one woman." As it was for my long-departed mother, there can be only one mate for me.

So while I feel the shortness of time left to me more in autumn than in any other time of the year, it does not cause me to surrender, but rather to "seek, find, and not to yield."

True I bravely say all this, but deep down I know every October finds me weaker than the one before, and that one of them will be my last. But I have determined, like Dylan Thomas's persona, to "Rage, rage against the dying of the light."

She did not put the book down until she had finished it, for it now represented all that she had lost. Perversely, she had even hoped to find flaws in his reasoning, for such flaws might bring a modicum of absolution for her treatment of him. Instead, she found herself in wholehearted agreement with what he had to say. She found herself looking up to him, admiring him in a way she had not believed possible, and realizing that, compared to him, she had been living only a half-life. Did she even know who she was? When was the last time she'd asked Life's Three Eternal Questions: *Who am I? Where have I come from? Where am I going?*

It was only after she had closed the book, turned off the light, and lay there listening to the rain that the truth came to her. She was anything but the first to discover that respect is the only true road to love. Love may precede respect, but love cannot survive the loss of it. The book had permitted her to see not only John's soul but her own naked soul as well, and it had revealed to her that she *loved* him—too late to be able to do anything about it. Finally, in torment and weariness, she knelt down by the bed and prayed this heartfelt prayer, childlike in its simplicity:

"Dear Lord, I love him. In my ignorance, I drove him away. But I want him, I want him to love me more than I've ever wanted anything in life. I don't know how I can find him, Lord, but You know where he is. If it be Your will—and how I hope it is!—would You be willing to awaken him, wherever he is tonight, and tell him that I am broken without him: incomplete, empty, and lonely. That my heart cries for him. Tell him to come for me, please? Thank you, Lord. Amen."

Then she just let go and dropped off to sleep listening to the rain slashing against her window, the wail of the wind, and the sad music of her heart.

4

The sea awoke at midnight from its sleep
    And round the pebbly beaches far and
    wide I heard the first wave of the rising tide
    Rush onward with uninterrupted sweep;
A voice out of the silence of the deep,
    A sound mysteriously multiplied
    As of a cataract from the mountain's side,
    Or roar of winds upon a wooded steep.
So comes to us at times, from the unknown
    And inaccessible solitudes of being,
    The rushing of the sea-tides of the soul;
And inspirations that we deem our own,
    Are some divine foreshadowing
        and foreseeing
    Of things beyond our reason or control.
        —"The Sound of the Sea,"
        by Henry Wadsworth Longfellow

John had remained in Camden, without really knowing why. He was restless yet unable to decide where to go next. In and out of his thoughts and dreams, appeared, disappeared, and reappeared the ever changing face of Eve. He had thought when she angrily stormed out that it was over, just another in a long line of romantic interludes, each enriching his life with the realization that he was loved after all. When each relationship ended, he resumed his aloneness with a sigh of relief—all but with this one. There was something about Eve that warmed his soul, that rekindled the embers in his heart, that held off sleep. That "something" refused to be ignored or reasoned away. Could it possibly be? After all the long years, here in the autumn of his life, could love have come at last? And at the cruelest of times—now that he knew how very little time he had left? His thoughts went back to his doctor's words, just two weeks before: "Your lab reports came back today, John, and the news isn't good. It's cancer and inoperable. You don't have much time left. Maybe three months, maybe six, maybe as long as a year. Only a miracle can grant you more."

And now *this!* But then he remembered: Eve's final words certainly provided no indication she felt the same about him.

Three evenings after Eve had left Camden, John sat in the inn lobby watching the ominous forecast. The hurricane now had a name, Teresa, and had reached wind velocity of well over 150 miles per hour. It was moving steadily north, having already flattened Bermuda. Unless it changed course it would smite Bar Harbor within sixty hours—*Bar Harbor,* where stood the closest thing to a home John's wandering life permitted. But he wasn't worried about it. The "castle" had stone walls eighteen inches thick; nothing short of an earthquake would threaten *it.* Suddenly the thought hit him: *If indeed my life is almost over, what damage could a hurricane possibly do to me? In fact, it'll most likely be my last one. I think I'll go home and ride it out. What an experience this promises to be!*

Several hours later he went to bed, but sleep didn't come until around midnight. At 2:05 A.M. he awoke. In an instant, he was wide awake. As clearly as though someone were talking to him in the room came these words:

EVE IS CALLING TO YOU. SHE LOVES YOU.

Life means little to her without you.

Her heart is broken.

John *knew* such a message could come from only one source. He got out of bed and knelt down: "Lord, if Eve loves me, I'm ever so grateful. But look at what Dr. Martin told me: My race is almost run, my life almost over—what could I give Eve but sorrow and heartbreak?"

Then came these words: MY CHILD, LEAVE ALL THAT TO ME, THE I AM, WHO KNOWS THE END FROM THE BEGINNING. GO TO HER.

He got up from his knees, turned on the light, and searched for the tour bus itinerary he had wheedled out of Eve's driver. She'd be in Bar Harbor by nightfall, leaving the group at least twenty-four hours to avoid the hurricane.

Well, sleep being impossible, I might as well pack up and get going, John thought.

5

O, weary hearts! O, slumbering eyes!
O, drooping souls, whose destinies
    Are fraught with fear and pain,
    Ye shall be loved again!

No one is so accursed by fate,
No one so utterly desolate,
    But some heart, though unknown
    Responds unto his own.

Responds,—as if, with unseen wings,
  An angel touched its quivering strings;
    And whispers, in its song,
      Where hast thou stayed so long?"
        —from "Endymion,"
          by Henry Wadsworth Longfellow

A strange peace filled Eve's heart as the bus slowly made its way to Bar Harbor. With every hour the wind and rain increased. The New York dispatch instructed the driver to go on to Bar Harbor as scheduled, but they would have to leave by 5:00 A.M. the next morning and take a long swing west before turning back toward the south.

Eve felt a strange sense of powerlessness overcome her. Since nothing she could do would change her present situation, she saw little reason to question or fight it. She had turned everything over to God—whatever was His will would be: either John would come, or he would not. Regardless, she knew now that she would love him always.

At long last, the bus came to a stop under the hotel portico. Eve, wishing to delay as long as possible the moment of reckoning, was the last to get off. Retrieving her suitcases, she walked into the warm, dry lobby. She scanned the room, but *he* was not there. So devastated was she by his absence that she felt the strength go out of her legs. In a mist of hopelessness and shattered dreams, she groped her way to a chair by the fireplace.

Suddenly she sensed rather than felt a presence behind her, and she stiffened as a well-remembered voice posed a question:

"Is Ms. LeBlanc ready for dinner?"

She swirled around in joyful disbelief, for there *he* stood! Not trusting speech with her heart pounding so, she could only nod. She looked at him, her parched heart drinking him in. Shyly she asked the most inane question, her heart in her eyes:

"So you found me."

"Yes, dear."

"Did you know I called to you last night?"

"Yes, dear."

"How?"

"God told me. Woke me up at five after two."

"What did God tell you?"

"Told me that your heart was broken, that you loved me, and that you were calling me."

"Did He even tell you how to *find* me?" she asked, incredulously.

He smiled that slightly impish smile she'd grown to love, and answered, "No, the good Lord expected me to use the brain He gave me and find out for myself."

"And you came after me, even though I'd been so despicable to you?"

"Yes, dear."

"Was it hard to do?"

"No, dear; no road could ever be hard to take with you at the end of it."

She could only shyly say, "I'm so glad you found me."

"Why?" his eyes teased.

"You know why."

"Yes, I do, but I want to hear you say it."

"I love you, John. But not until I read *October Song* did I realize how much. My home is wherever you are and could never be where you are not. I know it's shameless to tell you how much I love you before you tell me—"

He did not permit her to finish her sentence, for his arms engulfed her, and his tender kisses answered her unspoken question. Finally, he stepped back, still holding her.

But Eve had two more questions for him. "John, at Camden you told me that you didn't have much time left. What did you mean by that?"

He told her—every one of the doctor's words. Her face blanched during the telling.

Then she asked her second question: "John, will you marry me—tonight?"

"Tonight?"

Demurely, her lips curled adorably, she continued, "Yes, tonight. What was it you wrote in *October Song*? Something about not having time for 'the waiting game'?"

Words being superfluous at this point, again he let his arms and lips do the talking.

———————

Much later, as they stood together in one of the castle's arched porticos, watching the ten-foot breakers thundering in, precursors of much higher ones tomorrow, he tenderly lifted her chin and asked, "And you're not afraid?"

"Not with you, John. Not ever with you. And I'll pray each hour that God will spare you for me. But, even if the answer is no"—and here her eyes misted over, and her voice shook—"yes, even should the answer be no, my cup of joy will remain full, for time is irrelevant with love like ours."

"Eve?"

"Yes, darling?"

"Do you want to know what else God told me?"

"Of course!"

"He said," slowly repeating the words from memory: "My child, leave all that to Me, the I Am, who knows the end from the beginning. Go to her."

On his chest, tears raining down, she couldn't say a word. Didn't have to.

Just before going indoors, John asked her, "Well, Mrs. Baldwin, your brow is still a tad crinkled; is there yet another unasked question in your arsenal?"

Laughing joyously, all worries, all sorrows, forgotten, she admitted, "Yes, dear, one third, and last, and rather silly question."

"And what might that be, my dearest Eve?"

"What does the middle initial *A* stand for in your name?"

"You'll laugh."

"I won't either. Cross my heart—just try me."

"All right, I'll tell you. It's...Adam."

"Adam!" She rocked in a vain attempt to keep her promise, then laughed until she was too weak to stand: "Oh, Adam, Adam, I knew we'd have to start all over again at the beginning—but isn't this just a little ridiculous?"

ACKNOWLEDGMENTS

Introduction: "God's Great Gift—Tough Times," by Joseph Leininger Wheeler. Copyright 2000. Printed by permission of the author.

PART I: HEARTACHE

"Alone, Yet Not Alone Am I," by Henry Melchior Muhlenberg with Regina Leininger and Maria Le Roy. Special thanks to the Leininger Family newsletters and the archives of Pennsylvania.

"The Death Disk," by Mark Twain (Samuel Langhorne Clemens). First published in 1901.

"Two Candles for St. Anthony," by Arthur Milward. Printed by permission of the author.

"Quality," by John Galsworthy. Published in *The Inn of Tranquility*, Charles Scribner's Sons, 1912.

"A Good Name or Great Riches," by Frank Hampton. If anyone can provide knowledge of earliest publication date and publisher of this old story, please relay that information to Joe Wheeler (P.O. Box 1246, Conifer, CO 80433).

"The Circle of Fire" by Leonard C. Lee. Published in February 14, 1956, *Signs of the Times.* Reprinted by permission of Joe Wheeler and Pacific Press, Nampa, Idaho. If anyone can provide knowledge of author or descendant, please relay that information to Joe Wheeler (P.O. Box 1246, Conifer, CO 80433).

PART II: HOPE

"The Missing Word" by G. E. Wallace. Published in April 25, 1939, *The Youth's Instructor.* Reprinted by permission of Joe Wheeler (P.O. Box 1246, Conifer, CO 80433) and Review and Herald Publishing Association, Hagerstown, MD.

"The Red Geranium," by Viola M. Payne. Published in June 1, 1965, *The Youth's Instructor.* Reprinted by permission of Joe Wheeler and Review and Herald Publishing Association, Hagerstown, MD. If anyone can provide knowledge of author or descendants, please relay that information to Joe Wheeler (P.O. Box 1246, Conifer, CO 80433).

"Hilda's Trousseau" by Florence Crannell Means. Published in October 5, 1926, *The Youth's Instructor.* Reprinted by permission of Joe Wheeler and Review and Herald Publishing Association, Hagerstown, MD. If anyone can provide knowledge of author or descendants, please relay that information to Joe Wheeler (P.O. Box 1246, Conifer, CO 80433).

"158 Spruce Street," author unknown. If anyone can provide knowledge of authorship, earliest publication date, and publisher of this old story, please relay that information to Joe Wheeler (P.O. Box 1246, Conifer, CO 80433).

"Along Came Cynthia," by Harriet Lummis Smith. Published in
April 26, 1933, *Young People's Weekly.* Reprinted by permission of
Joe Wheeler (P.O. Box 1246, Conifer, CO 80433) and David C.
Cook Ministries, Colorado.

"My Son—Handicapped," author unknown. If anyone can provide
knowledge of authorship, earliest publication date, and publisher of
this story, please relay that information to Joe Wheeler (P.O. Box
1246, Conifer, CO 80433).

"Her Inside Face" by Beth Bradford Gilchrist. Published in March 29,
1927, *The Youth's Instructor.* Reprinted by permission of Joe Wheeler
and Review and Herald Publishing Association, Hagerstown, MD.
If anyone can provide knowledge of author or descendants, please
relay that information to Joe Wheeler (P.O. Box 1246, Conifer, CO
80433).

"The Dissolving of a Partnership," by Abbie Farwell Brown. Published
in September 1902 *The Ladies' World.*

PART III: HEALING

"A Message from the Sea," by Arthur Gordon. Published in January
1962 in *Guideposts.* Reprinted by permission of the author.

"The Making of Mike," by Irving Bacheller. If anyone can provide
knowledge of earliest publication date and publisher of this old
story, please relay that information to Joe Wheeler (P.O. Box 1246,
Conifer, CO 80433).

"The Wall of Silence," by Shirley Barksdale. Published in November/ December 1997, *Virtue*. Reprinted by permission of the author.

"The Ragged Cloak," by Margaret E. Sangster Jr. If anyone can provide knowledge of earliest publication date and publisher of this old story, please relay that information to Joe Wheeler (P.O. Box 1246, Conifer, CO 80433).

"The Firing of Donald Capen," by Alice Louise Lee. Published in December 26, 1907, *The Youth's Companion*.

"October Song," by Joseph Leininger Wheeler. Copyright © 2000. Printed by permission of the author.